DICTIONARY
THEME-BASED

British English Collection

ENGLISH-
ALBANIAN

The most useful words
To expand your lexicon and sharpen
your language skills

5000 words

Theme-based dictionary British English-Albanian - 5000 words

By Andrey Taranov

T&P Books vocabularies are intended for helping you learn, memorize and review foreign words. The dictionary is divided into themes, covering all major spheres of everyday activities, business, science, culture, etc.

The process of learning words using T&P Books' theme-based dictionaries gives you the following advantages:

- Correctly grouped source information predetermines success at subsequent stages of word memorization
- Availability of words derived from the same root allowing memorization of word units (rather than separate words)
- Small units of words facilitate the process of establishing associative links needed for consolidation of vocabulary
- Level of language knowledge can be estimated by the number of learned words

T&P Books Publishing
www.tpbooks.com

This book is also available in E-book formats.
Please visit www.tpbooks.com or the major online bookstores.

ALBANIAN THEME-BASED DICTIONARY
British English collection

T&P Books vocabularies are intended to help you learn, memorize, and review foreign words. The vocabulary contains over 5000 commonly used words arranged thematically.

- Vocabulary contains the most commonly used words
- Recommended as an addition to any language course
- Meets the needs of beginners and advanced learners of foreign languages
- Convenient for daily use, revision sessions, and self-testing activities
- Allows you to assess your vocabulary

Special features of the vocabulary

- Words are organized according to their meaning, not alphabetically
- Words are presented in three columns to facilitate the reviewing and self-testing processes
- Words in groups are divided into small blocks to facilitate the learning process
- The vocabulary offers a convenient and simple transcription of each foreign word

The vocabulary has 155 topics including:

Basic Concepts, Numbers, Colors, Months, Seasons, Units of Measurement, Clothing & Accessories, Food & Nutrition, Restaurant, Family Members, Relatives, Character, Feelings, Emotions, Diseases, City, Town, Sightseeing, Shopping, Money, House, Home, Office, Working in the Office, Import & Export, Marketing, Job Search, Sports, Education, Computer, Internet, Tools, Nature, Countries, Nationalities and more ...

TABLE OF CONTENTS

PRONUNCIATION GUIDE

T&P phonetic alphabet	Albanian example	English example
[a]	flas [flas]	shorter than in 'ask'
[e], [ɛ]	melodi [mɛlodí]	absent, pet
[ə]	kërkoj [kərkój]	driver, teacher
[i]	pikë [píkə]	shorter than in 'feet'
[o]	motor [motór]	pod, John
[u]	fuqi [fucí]	book
[y]	myshk [myʃk]	fuel, tuna
[b]	brakë [brákə]	baby, book
[c]	oqean [ocɛán]	Irish - ceist
[d]	adoptoj [adoptój]	day, doctor
[ʣ]	lexoj [lɛdzój]	beads, kids
[ʤ]	xham [dʒam]	joke, general
[ð]	dhomë [ðómə]	weather, together
[f]	i fortë [i fórtə]	face, food
[g]	bullgari [buɫgarí]	game, gold
[h]	jaht [jáht]	home, have
[j]	hyrje [hýrjɛ]	yes, New York
[ɟ]	zgjedh [zɟɛð]	geese
[k]	korik [korík]	clock, kiss
[l]	lëviz [ləvíz]	lace, people
[ɫ]	shkallë [ʃkáɫə]	feel
[m]	medalje [mɛdáljɛ]	magic, milk
[n]	klan [klan]	name, normal
[ɲ]	spanjoll [spaɲóɫ]	canyon, new
[ŋ]	trung [truŋ]	ring
[p]	polici [politsí]	pencil, private
[r]	i erët [i érət]	rice, radio
[ɾ]	groshë [gróʃə]	Spanish - pero
[s]	spital [spitál]	city, boss
[ʃ]	shes [ʃɛs]	machine, shark
[t]	tapet [tapét]	tourist, trip
[ʦ]	batica [batítsa]	cats, tsetse fly
[ʧ]	kaçube [katʃúbɛ]	church, French
[v]	javor [javór]	very, river
[z]	horizont [horizónt]	zebra, please
[ʒ]	kuzhinë [kuʒínə]	forge, pleasure
[θ]	përkthej [pərkθéj]	month, tooth

ABBREVIATIONS
used in the dictionary

English abbreviations

ab.	-	about
adj	-	adjective
adv	-	adverb
anim.	-	animate
as adj	-	attributive noun used as adjective
e.g.	-	for example
etc.	-	et cetera
fam.	-	familiar
fem.	-	feminine
form.	-	formal
inanim.	-	inanimate
masc.	-	masculine
math	-	mathematics
mil.	-	military
n	-	noun
pl	-	plural
pron.	-	pronoun
sb	-	somebody
sing.	-	singular
sth	-	something
v aux	-	auxiliary verb
vi	-	intransitive verb
vi, vt	-	intransitive, transitive verb
vt	-	transitive verb

Albanian abbreviations

f	-	feminine noun
m	-	masculine noun
pl	-	plural

BASIC CONCEPTS

Basic concepts. Part 1

1. Pronouns

I, me	Unë, mua	[unə], [múa]
you	ti, ty	[ti], [ty]
he	ai	[aí]
she	ajo	[ajó]
it	ai	[aí]
we	ne	[nɛ]
you (to a group)	ju	[ju]
they (masc.)	ata	[atá]
they (fem.)	ato	[ató]

2. Greetings. Salutations. Farewells

Hello! (fam.)	Përshëndetje!	[pərʃəndétjɛ!]
Hello! (form.)	Përshëndetje!	[pərʃəndétjɛ!]
Good morning!	Mirëmëngjes!	[mirəmənɟés!]
Good afternoon!	Mirëdita!	[mirədíta!]
Good evening!	Mirëmbrëma!	[mirəmbrə́ma!]
to say hello	përshëndes	[pərʃəndés]
Hi! (hello)	Ç'kemi!	[tʃkémi!]
greeting (n)	përshëndetje (f)	[pərʃəndétjɛ]
to greet (vt)	përshëndes	[pərʃəndés]
How are you? (form.)	Si jeni?	[si jéni?]
How are you? (fam.)	Si je?	[si jɛ?]
What's new?	Çfarë ka të re?	[tʃfárə ká tə ré?]
Goodbye!	Mirupafshim!	[mirupáfʃim!]
Bye!	U pafshim!	[u páfʃim!]
See you soon!	Shihemi së shpejti!	[ʃíhɛmi sə ʃpéjti!]
Farewell!	Lamtumirë!	[lamtumírə!]
to say goodbye	përshëndetem	[pərʃəndétɛm]
Cheers!	Tungjatjeta!	[tunɟatjéta!]
Thank you! Cheers!	Faleminderit!	[falɛmindérit!]
Thank you very much!	Faleminderit shumë!	[falɛmindérit ʃúmə!]
My pleasure!	Të lutem	[tə lútɛm]
Don't mention it!	Asgjë!	[asɟé!]
It was nothing	Asgjë	[asɟə́]

11

Excuse me! (fam.)	Më fal!	[mə fal!]
Excuse me! (form.)	Më falni!	[mə fálni!]
to excuse (forgive)	fal	[fal]

to apologize (vi)	kërkoj falje	[kərkój fáljɛ]
My apologies	Kërkoj ndjesë	[kərkój ndjésə]
I'm sorry!	Më vjen keq!	[mə vjɛn kɛc!]
to forgive (vt)	fal	[fal]
It's okay! (that's all right)	S'ka gjë!	[s'ka ɟə!]
please (adv)	të lutem	[tə lútɛm]

Don't forget!	Mos harro!	[mos haró!]
Certainly!	Sigurisht!	[siguríʃt!]
Of course not!	Sigurisht që jo!	[siguríʃt cə jo!]
Okay! (I agree)	Në rregull!	[nə réguɫ!]
That's enough!	Mjafton!	[mjaftón!]

3. How to address

Excuse me, ...	Më falni, ...	[mə fálni, ...]
mister, sir	zotëri	[zotərí]
madam	zonjë	[zóɲə]
miss	zonjushë	[zoɲúʃə]
young man	djalë i ri	[djálə i rí]
young man (little boy)	djalosh	[djalóʃ]
miss (little girl)	vajzë	[vájzə]

4. Cardinal numbers. Part 1

0 zero	zero	[zéro]
1 one	një	[ɲə]
2 two	dy	[dy]
3 three	tre	[trɛ]
4 four	katër	[kátər]

5 five	pesë	[pésə]
6 six	gjashtë	[ɟáʃtə]
7 seven	shtatë	[ʃtátə]
8 eight	tetë	[tétə]
9 nine	nëntë	[nəntə]

10 ten	dhjetë	[ðjétə]
11 eleven	njëmbëdhjetë	[ɲəmbəðjétə]
12 twelve	dymbëdhjetë	[dymbəðjétə]
13 thirteen	trembëdhjetë	[trɛmbəðjétə]
14 fourteen	katërmbëdhjetë	[katərmbəðjétə]

15 fifteen	pesëmbëdhjetë	[pɛsəmbəðjétə]
16 sixteen	gjashtëmbëdhjetë	[ɟaʃtəmbəðjétə]
17 seventeen	shtatëmbëdhjetë	[ʃtatəmbəðjétə]
18 eighteen	tetëmbëdhjetë	[tɛtəmbəðjétə]
19 nineteen	nëntëmbëdhjetë	[nəntəmbəðjétə]

20 twenty	njëzet	[ɲəzét]
21 twenty-one	njëzet e një	[ɲəzét ɛ ɲə]
22 twenty-two	njëzet e dy	[ɲəzét ɛ dy]
23 twenty-three	njëzet e tre	[ɲəzét ɛ trɛ]

30 thirty	tridhjetë	[triðjétə]
31 thirty-one	tridhjetë e një	[triðjétə ɛ ɲə]
32 thirty-two	tridhjetë e dy	[triðjétə ɛ dy]
33 thirty-three	tridhjetë e tre	[triðjétə ɛ trɛ]

40 forty	dyzet	[dyzét]
41 forty-one	dyzet e një	[dyzét ɛ ɲə]
42 forty-two	dyzet e dy	[dyzét ɛ dy]
43 forty-three	dyzet e tre	[dyzét ɛ trɛ]

50 fifty	pesëdhjetë	[pɛsəðjétə]
51 fifty-one	pesëdhjetë e një	[pɛsəðjétə ɛ ɲə]
52 fifty-two	pesëdhjetë e dy	[pɛsəðjétə ɛ dy]
53 fifty-three	pesëdhjetë e tre	[pɛsəðjétə ɛ trɛ]

60 sixty	gjashtëdhjetë	[ɟaʃtəðjétə]
61 sixty-one	gjashtëdhjetë e një	[ɟaʃtəðjétə ɛ ɲə]
62 sixty-two	gjashtëdhjetë e dy	[ɟaʃtəðjétə ɛ dý]
63 sixty-three	gjashtëdhjetë e tre	[ɟaʃtəðjétə ɛ tré]

70 seventy	shtatëdhjetë	[ʃtatəðjétə]
71 seventy-one	shtatëdhjetë e një	[ʃtatəðjétə ɛ ɲə]
72 seventy-two	shtatëdhjetë e dy	[ʃtatəðjétə ɛ dy]
73 seventy-three	shtatëdhjetë e tre	[ʃtatəðjétə ɛ trɛ]

80 eighty	tetëdhjetë	[tɛtəðjétə]
81 eighty-one	tetëdhjetë e një	[tɛtəðjétə ɛ ɲə]
82 eighty-two	tetëdhjetë e dy	[tɛtəðjétə ɛ dy]
83 eighty-three	tetëdhjetë e tre	[tɛtəðjétə ɛ trɛ]

90 ninety	nëntëdhjetë	[nəntəðjétə]
91 ninety-one	nëntëdhjetë e një	[nəntəðjétə ɛ ɲə]
92 ninety-two	nëntëdhjetë e dy	[nəntəðjétə ɛ dy]
93 ninety-three	nëntëdhjetë e tre	[nəntəðjétə ɛ trɛ]

5. Cardinal numbers. Part 2

100 one hundred	njëqind	[ɲəcínd]
200 two hundred	dyqind	[dycínd]
300 three hundred	treqind	[trɛcínd]
400 four hundred	katërqind	[katərcínd]
500 five hundred	pesëqind	[pɛsəcínd]

600 six hundred	gjashtëqind	[ɟaʃtəcínd]
700 seven hundred	shtatëqind	[ʃtatəcínd]
800 eight hundred	tetëqind	[tɛtəcínd]
900 nine hundred	nëntëqind	[nəntəcínd]
1000 one thousand	një mijë	[ɲə míjə]
2000 two thousand	dy mijë	[dy míjə]

3000 three thousand	**tre mijë**	[trɛ míjə]
10000 ten thousand	**dhjetë mijë**	[ðjétə míjə]
one hundred thousand	**njëqind mijë**	[ɲəcínd míjə]
million	**milion** (m)	[milión]
billion	**miliardë** (f)	[miliárdə]

6. Ordinal numbers

first (adj)	**i pari**	[i pári]
second (adj)	**i dyti**	[i dýti]
third (adj)	**i treti**	[i tréti]
fourth (adj)	**i katërti**	[i kátərti]
fifth (adj)	**i pesti**	[i pésti]
sixth (adj)	**i gjashti**	[i ɟáʃti]
seventh (adj)	**i shtati**	[i ʃtáti]
eighth (adj)	**i teti**	[i téti]
ninth (adj)	**i nënti**	[i nénti]
tenth (adj)	**i dhjeti**	[i ðjéti]

7. Numbers. Fractions

fraction	**thyesë** (f)	[θýɛsə]
one half	**gjysma**	[ɟýsma]
one third	**një e treta**	[ɲə ɛ tréta]
one quarter	**një e katërta**	[ɲə ɛ kátərta]
one eighth	**një e teta**	[ɲə ɛ téta]
one tenth	**një e dhjeta**	[ɲə ɛ ðjéta]
two thirds	**dy të tretat**	[dy tə trétat]
three quarters	**tre të katërtat**	[trɛ tə kátərtat]

8. Numbers. Basic operations

subtraction	**zbritje** (f)	[zbrítjɛ]
to subtract (vi, vt)	**zbres**	[zbrɛs]
division	**pjesëtim** (m)	[pjɛsətím]
to divide (vt)	**pjesëtoj**	[pjɛsətój]
addition	**mbledhje** (f)	[mbléðjɛ]
to add up (vt)	**shtoj**	[ʃtoj]
to add (vi)	**mbledh**	[mbléð]
multiplication	**shumëzim** (m)	[ʃuməzím]
to multiply (vt)	**shumëzoj**	[ʃuməzój]

9. Numbers. Miscellaneous

digit, figure	**shifër** (f)	[ʃífər]
number	**numër** (m)	[númər]

numeral	numerik (m)	[numɛrík]
minus sign	minus (m)	[minús]
plus sign	plus (m)	[plus]
formula	formulë (f)	[formúlə]

calculation	llogaritje (f)	[ɬogarítjɛ]
to count (vi, vt)	numëroj	[numərój]
to count up	llogaris	[ɬogarís]
to compare (vt)	krahasoj	[krahasój]

How much?	Sa?	[sa?]
sum, total	shuma (f)	[ʃúma]
result	rezultat (m)	[rɛzultát]
remainder	mbetje (f)	[mbétjɛ]

a few (e.g., ~ years ago)	disa	[disá]
little (I had ~ time)	pak	[pak]
few (I have ~ friends)	disa	[disá]
a little (~ water)	pak	[pak]
the rest	mbetje (f)	[mbétjɛ]
one and a half	një e gjysmë (f)	[ɲə ɛ ɟýsmə]
dozen	dyzinë (f)	[dyzínə]

in half (adv)	përgjysmë	[pərɟýsmə]
equally (evenly)	gjysmë për gjysmë	[ɟýsmə pər ɟýsmə]
half	gjysmë (f)	[ɟýsmə]
time (three ~s)	herë (f)	[hérə]

10. The most important verbs. Part 1

to advise (vt)	këshilloj	[kəʃiɬój]
to agree (say yes)	bie dakord	[bíɛ dakórd]
to answer (vi, vt)	përgjigjem	[pərɟíɟɛm]
to apologize (vi)	kërkoj falje	[kərkój fáljɛ]
to arrive (vi)	arrij	[aríj]

to ask (~ oneself)	pyes	[pýɛs]
to ask (~ sb to do sth)	pyes	[pýɛs]
to be (vi)	jam	[jam]

to be afraid	kam frikë	[kam fríkə]
to be hungry	kam uri	[kam urí]
to be interested in ...	interesohem ...	[intɛrɛsóhɛm ...]
to be needed	nevojitet	[nɛvojítɛt]
to be surprised	çuditem	[tʃudítɛm]

to be thirsty	kam etje	[kam étjɛ]
to begin (vt)	filloj	[fiɬój]
to belong to ...	përkas ...	[pərkás ...]
to boast (vi)	mburrem	[mbúrɛm]
to break (split into pieces)	ndahem	[ndáhɛm]
to call (~ for help)	thërras	[θərás]
can (v aux)	mund	[mund]
to catch (vt)	kap	[kap]

to change (vt)	ndryshoj	[ndryʃój]
to choose (select)	zgjedh	[zɟɛð]
to come down (the stairs)	zbres	[zbrɛs]
to compare (vt)	krahasoj	[krahasój]
to complain (vi, vt)	ankohem	[ankóhɛm]
to confuse (mix up)	ngatërroj	[ŋatərój]
to continue (vt)	vazhdoj	[vaʒdój]
to control (vt)	kontrolloj	[kontroɫój]
to cook (dinner)	gatuaj	[gatúaj]
to cost (vt)	kushton	[kuʃtón]
to count (add up)	numëroj	[numərój]
to count on ...	mbështetem ...	[mbəʃtétɛm ...]
to create (vt)	krijoj	[krijój]
to cry (weep)	qaj	[caj]

11. The most important verbs. Part 2

to deceive (vi, vt)	mashtroj	[maʃtrój]
to decorate (tree, street)	zbukuroj	[zbukurój]
to defend (a country, etc.)	mbroj	[mbrój]
to demand (request firmly)	kërkoj	[kərkój]
to dig (vt)	gërmoj	[gərmój]
to discuss (vt)	diskutoj	[diskutój]
to do (vt)	bëj	[bəj]
to doubt (have doubts)	dyshoj	[dyʃój]
to drop (let fall)	lëshoj	[ləʃój]
to enter (room, house, etc.)	hyj	[hyj]
to excuse (forgive)	fal	[fal]
to exist (vi)	ekzistoj	[ɛkzistój]
to expect (foresee)	parashikoj	[paraʃikój]
to explain (vt)	shpjegoj	[ʃpjɛgój]
to fall (vi)	bie	[bíɛ]
to fancy (vt)	pëlqej	[pəlcéj]
to find (vt)	gjej	[ɟéj]
to finish (vt)	përfundoj	[pərfundój]
to fly (vi)	fluturoj	[fluturój]
to follow ... (come after)	ndjek ...	[ndjék ...]
to forget (vi, vt)	harroj	[harój]
to forgive (vt)	fal	[fal]
to give (vt)	jap	[jap]
to give a hint	aludoj	[aludój]
to go (on foot)	ec në këmbë	[ɛts nə kémbə]
to go for a swim	notoj	[notój]
to go out (for dinner, etc.)	dal	[dal]
to guess (the answer)	hamendësoj	[hamɛndəsój]
to have (vt)	kam	[kam]
to have breakfast	ha mëngjes	[ha məɲés]

to have dinner	ha darkë	[ha dárkə]
to have lunch	ha drekë	[ha drékə]
to hear (vt)	dëgjoj	[dəɟój]

to help (vt)	ndihmoj	[ndihmój]
to hide (vt)	fsheh	[fʃéh]
to hope (vi, vt)	shpresoj	[ʃprɛsój]
to hunt (vi, vt)	dal për gjah	[dál pər ɟáh]
to hurry (vi)	nxitoj	[ndzitój]

12. The most important verbs. Part 3

to inform (vt)	informoj	[informój]
to insist (vi, vt)	këmbëngul	[kəmbəŋúl]
to insult (vt)	fyej	[fýɛj]
to invite (vt)	ftoj	[ftoj]
to joke (vi)	bëj shaka	[bəj ʃaká]

to keep (vt)	mbaj	[mbáj]
to keep silent, to hush	hesht	[hɛʃt]
to kill (vt)	vras	[vras]
to know (sb)	njoh	[ɲóh]
to know (sth)	di	[di]
to laugh (vi)	qesh	[cɛʃ]

to liberate (city, etc.)	çliroj	[tʃlirój]
to look for … (search)	kërkoj …	[kərkój …]
to love (sb)	dashuroj	[daʃurój]
to make a mistake	gaboj	[gabój]
to manage, to run	drejtoj	[drɛjtój]
to mean (signify)	nënkuptoj	[nənkuptój]
to mention (talk about)	përmend	[pərménd]
to miss (school, etc.)	humbas	[humbás]
to notice (see)	vërej	[vəréj]
to object (vi, vt)	kundërshtoj	[kundərʃtój]

to observe (see)	vëzhgoj	[vəʒgój]
to open (vt)	hap	[hap]
to order (meal, etc.)	porosis	[porosís]
to order (mil.)	urdhëroj	[urðərój]
to own (possess)	zotëroj	[zotərój]

to participate (vi)	marr pjesë	[mar pjésə]
to pay (vi, vt)	paguaj	[pagúaj]
to permit (vt)	lejoj	[lɛjój]
to plan (vt)	planifikoj	[planifikój]
to play (children)	luaj	[lúaj]

to pray (vi, vt)	lutem	[lútɛm]
to prefer (vt)	preferoj	[prɛfɛrój]
to promise (vt)	premtoj	[prɛmtój]
to pronounce (vt)	shqiptoj	[ʃciptój]
to propose (vt)	propozoj	[propozój]
to punish (vt)	ndëshkoj	[ndəʃkój]

13. The most important verbs. Part 4

to read (vi, vt)	lexoj	[lɛdzój]
to recommend (vt)	rekomandoj	[rɛkomandój]
to refuse (vi, vt)	refuzoj	[rɛfuzój]
to regret (be sorry)	pendohem	[pɛndóhɛm]
to rent (sth from sb)	marr me qira	[mar mɛ cirá]
to repeat (say again)	përsëris	[pərsərís]
to reserve, to book	rezervoj	[rɛzɛrvój]
to run (vi)	vrapoj	[vrapój]
to save (rescue)	shpëtoj	[ʃpətój]
to say (~ thank you)	them	[θɛm]
to scold (vt)	qortoj	[cortój]
to see (vt)	shikoj	[ʃikój]
to sell (vt)	shes	[ʃɛs]
to send (vt)	dërgoj	[dərgój]
to shoot (vi)	qëlloj	[cəɫój]
to shout (vi)	bërtas	[bərtás]
to show (vt)	tregoj	[trɛgój]
to sign (document)	nënshkruaj	[nənʃkrúaj]
to sit down (vi)	ulem	[úlɛm]
to smile (vi)	buzëqesh	[buzəcéʃ]
to speak (vi, vt)	flas	[flas]
to steal (money, etc.)	vjedh	[vjɛð]
to stop (for pause, etc.)	ndaloj	[ndalój]
to stop (please ~ calling me)	ndaloj	[ndalój]
to study (vt)	studioj	[studiój]
to swim (vi)	notoj	[notój]
to take (vt)	marr	[mar]
to think (vi, vt)	mendoj	[mɛndój]
to threaten (vt)	kërcënoj	[kərtsənój]
to touch (with hands)	prek	[prɛk]
to translate (vt)	përkthej	[pərkθéj]
to trust (vt)	besoj	[bɛsój]
to try (attempt)	përpiqem	[pərpícɛm]
to turn (e.g., ~ left)	kthej	[kθɛj]
to underestimate (vt)	nënvlerësoj	[nənvlɛrəsój]
to understand (vt)	kuptoj	[kuptój]
to unite (vt)	bashkoj	[baʃkój]
to wait (vt)	pres	[prɛs]
to want (wish, desire)	dëshiroj	[dəʃirój]
to warn (vt)	paralajmëroj	[paralajmərój]
to work (vi)	punoj	[punój]
to write (vt)	shkruaj	[ʃkrúaj]
to write down	mbaj shënim	[mbáj ʃəním]

14. Colours

colour	ngjyrë (f)	[ɲƴrə]
shade (tint)	nuancë (f)	[nuántsə]
hue	tonalitet (m)	[tonalitét]
rainbow	ylber (m)	[ylbér]

white (adj)	e bardhë	[ɛ bárðə]
black (adj)	e zezë	[ɛ zézə]
grey (adj)	gri	[gri]

green (adj)	jeshile	[jɛʃílɛ]
yellow (adj)	e verdhë	[ɛ vérðə]
red (adj)	e kuqe	[ɛ kúcɛ]

blue (adj)	blu	[blu]
light blue (adj)	bojëqielli	[bojəciéɫi]
pink (adj)	rozë	[rózə]
orange (adj)	portokalli	[portokáɫi]
violet (adj)	bojëvjollcë	[bojəvjóɫtsə]
brown (adj)	kafe	[káfɛ]

| golden (adj) | e artë | [ɛ ártə] |
| silvery (adj) | e argjendtë | [ɛ arɟéndtə] |

beige (adj)	bezhë	[béʒə]
cream (adj)	krem	[krɛm]
turquoise (adj)	e bruztë	[ɛ brúztə]
cherry red (adj)	qershi	[cɛrʃí]
lilac (adj)	jargavan	[jargaván]
crimson (adj)	e kuqe e thellë	[ɛ kúcɛ ɛ θéɫə]

light (adj)	e hapur	[ɛ hápur]
dark (adj)	e errët	[ɛ érət]
bright, vivid (adj)	e ndritshme	[ɛ ndrítʃmɛ]

coloured (pencils)	e ngjyrosur	[ɛ ɲɟyrósur]
colour (e.g. ~ film)	ngjyrë	[ɲƴrə]
black-and-white (adj)	bardhë e zi	[bárðə ɛ zi]
plain (one-coloured)	njëngjyrëshe	[ɲənɟýrəʃɛ]
multicoloured (adj)	shumëngjyrëshe	[ʃumənɟýrəʃɛ]

15. Questions

Who?	Kush?	[kuʃ?]
What?	Çka?	[tʃká?]
Where? (at, in)	Ku?	[ku?]
Where (to)?	Për ku?	[pər ku?]
From where?	Nga ku?	[ŋa ku?]
When?	Kur?	[kur?]
Why? (What for?)	Pse?	[psɛ?]
Why? (~ are you crying?)	Pse?	[psɛ?]
What for?	Për çfarë arsye?	[pər tʃfárə arsýɛ?]

How? (in what way)	Si?	[si?]
What? (What kind of ...?)	Çfarë?	[tʃfárə?]
Which?	Cili?	[tsíli?]

To whom?	Kujt?	[kújt?]
About whom?	Për kë?	[pər kə?]
About what?	Për çfarë?	[pər tʃfárə?]
With whom?	Me kë?	[mɛ kə?]

How many? How much?	Sa?	[sa?]
Whose?	Të kujt?	[tə kujt?]

16. Prepositions

with (accompanied by)	me	[mɛ]
without	pa	[pa]
to (indicating direction)	për në	[pər nə]
about (talking ~ ...)	për	[pər]
before (in time)	përpara	[pərpára]
in front of ...	para ...	[pára ...]

under (beneath, below)	nën	[nən]
above (over)	mbi	[mbí]
on (atop)	mbi	[mbí]
from (off, out of)	nga	[ŋa]
of (made from)	nga	[ŋa]

in (e.g. ~ ten minutes)	për	[pər]
over (across the top of)	sipër	[sípər]

17. Function words. Adverbs. Part 1

Where? (at, in)	Ku?	[ku?]
here (adv)	këtu	[kətú]
there (adv)	atje	[atjé]

somewhere (to be)	diku	[dikú]
nowhere (not in any place)	askund	[askúnd]

by (near, beside)	afër	[áfər]
by the window	tek dritarja	[tɛk dritárja]

Where (to)?	Për ku?	[pər ku?]
here (e.g. come ~!)	këtu	[kətú]
there (e.g. to go ~)	atje	[atjé]
from here (adv)	nga këtu	[ŋa kətú]
from there (adv)	nga atje	[ŋa atjɛ]

close (adv)	pranë	[pránə]
far (adv)	larg	[larg]
near (e.g. ~ Paris)	afër	[áfər]
nearby (adv)	pranë	[pránə]

not far (adv)	jo larg	[jo lárg]
left (adj)	majtë	[májtə]
on the left	majtas	[májtas]
to the left	në të majtë	[nə tə májtə]

right (adj)	djathtë	[djáθtə]
on the right	djathtas	[djáθtas]
to the right	në të djathtë	[nə tə djáθtə]

in front (adv)	përballë	[pərbáɫə]
front (as adj)	i përparmë	[i pərpármə]
ahead (the kids ran ~)	përpara	[pərpára]

behind (adv)	prapa	[prápa]
from behind	nga prapa	[ŋa prápa]
back (towards the rear)	pas	[pas]

| middle | mes (m) | [mɛs] |
| in the middle | në mes | [nə mɛs] |

at the side	në anë	[nə anə]
everywhere (adv)	kudo	[kúdo]
around (in all directions)	përreth	[pəréθ]

from inside	nga brenda	[ŋa brénda]
somewhere (to go)	diku	[dikú]
straight (directly)	drejt	[dréjt]
back (e.g. come ~)	pas	[pas]

| from anywhere | nga kudo | [ŋa kúdo] |
| from somewhere | nga diku | [ŋa dikú] |

firstly (adv)	së pari	[sə pári]
secondly (adv)	së dyti	[sə dýti]
thirdly (adv)	së treti	[sə tréti]

suddenly (adv)	befas	[béfas]
at first (in the beginning)	në fillim	[nə fiɫím]
for the first time	për herë të parë	[pər hérə tə párə]
long before ...	shumë përpara ...	[ʃúmə pərpára ...]
anew (over again)	sërish	[səríʃ]
for good (adv)	një herë e mirë	[ɲə hérə ɛ mírə]

never (adv)	kurrë	[kúrə]
again (adv)	përsëri	[pərsərí]
now (at present)	tani	[táni]
often (adv)	shpesh	[ʃpɛʃ]
then (adv)	atëherë	[atəhérə]
urgently (quickly)	urgjent	[urɟént]
usually (adv)	zakonisht	[zakoníʃt]

by the way, ...	meqë ra fjala, ...	[mécə ra fjála, ...]
possibly	ndoshta	[ndóʃta]
probably (adv)	mundësisht	[mundəsíʃt]
maybe (adv)	mbase	[mbásɛ]
besides ...	përveç	[pərvétʃ]

that's why ...	ja përse ...	[ja pərsé ...]
in spite of ...	pavarësisht se ...	[pavarəsíʃt sɛ ...]
thanks to ...	falë ...	[fálə ...]

what (pron.)	çfarë	[tʃfárə]
that (conj.)	që	[cə]
something	diçka	[ditʃká]
anything (something)	ndonji gjë	[ndoɲí ɟə]
nothing	asgjë	[asɟé]

who (pron.)	kush	[kuʃ]
someone	dikush	[dikúʃ]
somebody	dikush	[dikúʃ]

nobody	askush	[askúʃ]
nowhere (a voyage to ~)	askund	[askúnd]
nobody's	i askujt	[i askújt]
somebody's	i dikujt	[i dikújt]

so (I'm ~ glad)	aq	[ác]
also (as well)	gjithashtu	[ɟiθaʃtú]
too (as well)	gjithashtu	[ɟiθaʃtú]

18. Function words. Adverbs. Part 2

Why?	Pse?	[psɛ?]
for some reason	për një arsye	[pər ɲə arsýɛ]
because ...	sepse ...	[sɛpsé ...]
for some purpose	për ndonjë shkak	[pər ndóɲə ʃkak]

and	dhe	[ðɛ]
or	ose	[ósɛ]
but	por	[por]
for (e.g. ~ me)	për	[pər]

too (excessively)	tepër	[tépər]
only (exclusively)	vetëm	[vétəm]
exactly (adv)	pikërisht	[pikəríʃt]
about (more or less)	rreth	[rɛθ]

approximately (adv)	përafërsisht	[pərafərsíʃt]
approximate (adj)	përafërt	[pəráfərt]
almost (adv)	pothuajse	[poθúajsɛ]
the rest	mbetje (f)	[mbétjɛ]

the other (second)	tjetri	[tjétri]
other (different)	tjetër	[tjétər]
each (adj)	çdo	[tʃdo]
any (no matter which)	çfarëdo	[tʃfarədó]
many (adj)	disa	[disá]
much (adv)	shumë	[ʃúmə]
many people	shumë njerëz	[ʃúmə ɲérəz]
all (everyone)	të gjithë	[tə ɟíθə]
in return for ...	në vend të ...	[nə vénd tə ...]

in exchange (adv)	**në shkëmbim të ...**	[nə ʃkəmbím tə ...]
by hand (made)	**me dorë**	[mɛ dórə]
hardly (negative opinion)	**vështirë se ...**	[vəʃtírə sɛ ...]
probably (adv)	**mundësisht**	[mundəsíʃt]
on purpose (intentionally)	**me qëllim**	[mɛ cəɫím]
by accident (adv)	**aksidentalisht**	[aksidɛntalíʃt]
very (adv)	**shumë**	[ʃúmə]
for example (adv)	**për shembull**	[pər ʃémbuɫ]
between	**midis**	[midís]
among	**rreth**	[rɛθ]
so much (such a lot)	**kaq shumë**	[kác ʃúmə]
especially (adv)	**veçanërisht**	[vɛtʃanəríʃt]

Basic concepts. Part 2

Monday	E hënë (f)	[ɛ hénə]
Tuesday	E martë (f)	[ɛ mártə]
Wednesday	E mërkurë (f)	[ɛ mərkúrə]
Thursday	E enjte (f)	[ɛ éɲtɛ]
Friday	E premte (f)	[ɛ prémtɛ]
Saturday	E shtunë (f)	[ɛ ʃtúnə]
Sunday	E dielë (f)	[ɛ díɛlə]

today (adv)	sot	[sot]
tomorrow (adv)	nesër	[nésər]
the day after tomorrow	pasnesër	[pasnésər]
yesterday (adv)	dje	[djé]
the day before yesterday	pardje	[pardjé]

day	ditë (f)	[dítə]
working day	ditë pune (f)	[dítə púnɛ]
public holiday	festë kombëtare (f)	[féstə kombətárɛ]
day off	ditë pushim (m)	[dítə puʃím]
weekend	fundjavë (f)	[fundjávə]

all day long	gjithë ditën	[ɟíθə dítən]
the next day (adv)	ditën pasardhëse	[dítən pasárðəsɛ]
two days ago	dy ditë më parë	[dy dítə mə párə]
the day before	një ditë më parë	[ɲə dítə mə párə]
daily (adj)	ditor	[ditór]
every day (adv)	çdo ditë	[tʃdo dítə]

week	javë (f)	[jávə]
last week (adv)	javën e kaluar	[jávən ɛ kalúar]
next week (adv)	javën e ardhshme	[jávən ɛ árðʃmɛ]
weekly (adj)	javor	[javór]
every week (adv)	çdo javë	[tʃdo jávə]
twice a week	dy herë në javë	[dy hérə nə jávə]
every Tuesday	çdo të martë	[tʃdo tə mártə]

morning	mëngjes (m)	[mənɟés]
in the morning	në mëngjes	[nə mənɟés]
noon, midday	mesditë (f)	[mɛsdítə]
in the afternoon	pasdite	[pasdítɛ]

| evening | mbrëmje (f) | [mbrémjɛ] |
| in the evening | në mbrëmje | [nə mbrémjɛ] |

night	natë (f)	[nátə]
at night	natën	[nátən]
midnight	mesnatë (f)	[mɛsnátə]

second	sekondë (f)	[sɛkóndə]
minute	minutë (f)	[minútə]
hour	orë (f)	[órə]
half an hour	gjysmë ore (f)	[ɟýsmə órɛ]
a quarter-hour	çerek ore (m)	[ʧɛrék órɛ]
fifteen minutes	pesëmbëdhjetë minuta	[pɛsəmbəðjétə minúta]
24 hours	24 orë	[ɲəzét ɛ kátər órə]

sunrise	agim (m)	[agím]
dawn	agim (m)	[agím]
early morning	mëngjes herët (m)	[mənɟés hérət]
sunset	perëndim dielli (m)	[pɛrəndím diéɬi]

early in the morning	herët në mëngjes	[hérət nə mənɟés]
this morning	sot në mëngjes	[sot nə mənɟés]
tomorrow morning	nesër në mëngjes	[nésər nə mənɟés]

this afternoon	sot pasdite	[sot pasdítɛ]
in the afternoon	pasdite	[pasdítɛ]
tomorrow afternoon	nesër pasdite	[nésər pasdítɛ]

| tonight (this evening) | sonte në mbrëmje | [sóntɛ nə mbrəmjɛ] |
| tomorrow night | nesër në mbrëmje | [nésər nə mbrémjɛ] |

at 3 o'clock sharp	në orën 3 fiks	[nə órən trɛ fiks]
about 4 o'clock	rreth orës 4	[rɛθ órəs kátər]
by 12 o'clock	deri në orën 12	[déri nə órən dymbəðjétə]

in 20 minutes	për 20 minuta	[pər ɲəzét minúta]
in an hour	për një orë	[pər ɲə órə]
on time (adv)	në orar	[nə orár]

a quarter to ...	çerek ...	[ʧɛrék ...]
within an hour	brenda një ore	[brénda ɲə órɛ]
every 15 minutes	çdo 15 minuta	[ʧdo pɛsəmbəðjétə minúta]
round the clock	gjithë ditën	[ɟíθə dítən]

21. Months. Seasons

January	Janar (m)	[janár]
February	Shkurt (m)	[ʃkurt]
March	Mars (m)	[mars]
April	Prill (m)	[priɬ]
May	Maj (m)	[maj]
June	Qershor (m)	[cɛrʃór]

July	Korrik (m)	[korík]
August	Gusht (m)	[guʃt]
September	Shtator (m)	[ʃtatór]
October	Tetor (m)	[tɛtór]

| November | Nëntor (m) | [nəntór] |
| December | Dhjetor (m) | [ðjɛtór] |

spring	pranverë (f)	[pranvérə]
in spring	në pranverë	[nə pranvérə]
spring (as adj)	pranveror	[pranvɛrór]

summer	verë (f)	[vérə]
in summer	në verë	[nə vérə]
summer (as adj)	veror	[vɛrór]

autumn	vjeshtë (f)	[vjéʃtə]
in autumn	në vjeshtë	[nə vjéʃtə]
autumn (as adj)	vjeshtor	[vjéʃtor]

winter	dimër (m)	[dímər]
in winter	në dimër	[nə dímər]
winter (as adj)	dimëror	[dimərór]

month	muaj (m)	[múaj]
this month	këtë muaj	[kətə múaj]
next month	muajin tjetër	[múajin tjétər]
last month	muajin e kaluar	[múajin ɛ kalúar]

a month ago	para një muaji	[pára ɲə múaji]
in a month (a month later)	pas një muaji	[pas ɲə múaji]
in 2 months (2 months later)	pas dy muajsh	[pas dy múajʃ]
the whole month	gjithë muajin	[ɟíθə múajin]
all month long	gjatë gjithë muajit	[ɟátə ɟíθə múajit]

monthly (~ magazine)	mujor	[mujór]
monthly (adv)	mujor	[mujór]
every month	çdo muaj	[tʃdo múaj]
twice a month	dy herë në muaj	[dy hérə nə múaj]

year	vit (m)	[vit]
this year	këtë vit	[kətə vít]
next year	vitin tjetër	[vítin tjétər]
last year	vitin e kaluar	[vítin ɛ kalúar]

a year ago	para një viti	[pára ɲə víti]
in a year	për një vit	[pər ɲə vit]
in two years	për dy vite	[pər dy vítɛ]
the whole year	gjithë vitin	[ɟíθə vítin]
all year long	gjatë gjithë vitit	[ɟátə ɟíθə vítit]

every year	çdo vit	[tʃdo vít]
annual (adj)	vjetor	[vjɛtór]
annually (adv)	çdo vit	[tʃdo vít]
4 times a year	4 herë në vit	[kátər hérə nə vit]

date (e.g. today's ~)	datë (f)	[dátə]
date (e.g. ~ of birth)	data (f)	[dáta]
calendar	kalendar (m)	[kalɛndár]
half a year	gjysmë viti	[ɟýsmə víti]
six months	gjashtë muaj	[ɟáʃtə múaj]

| season (summer, etc.) | stinë (f) | [stínə] |
| century | shekull (m) | [ʃékuɫ] |

22. Units of measurement

weight	peshë (f)	[péʃə]
length	gjatësi (f)	[ɟatəsí]
width	gjerësi (f)	[ɟɛrəsí]
height	lartësi (f)	[lartəsí]
depth	thellësi (f)	[θɛɫəsí]
volume	vëllim (m)	[vəɫím]
area	sipërfaqe (f)	[sipərfácɛ]

gram	gram (m)	[gram]
milligram	miligram (m)	[miligrám]
kilogram	kilogram (m)	[kilográm]
ton	ton (m)	[ton]
pound	paund (m)	[páund]
ounce	ons (m)	[ons]

metre	metër (m)	[métər]
millimetre	milimetër (m)	[milimétər]
centimetre	centimetër (m)	[tsɛntimétər]
kilometre	kilometër (m)	[kilométər]
mile	milje (f)	[míljɛ]

inch	inç (m)	[intʃ]
foot	këmbë (f)	[kémbə]
yard	jard (m)	[járd]

| square metre | metër katror (m) | [métər katrór] |
| hectare | hektar (m) | [hɛktár] |

litre	litër (m)	[lítər]
degree	gradë (f)	[grádə]
volt	volt (m)	[volt]
ampere	amper (m)	[ampér]
horsepower	kuaj-fuqi (f)	[kúaj-fucí]

quantity	sasi (f)	[sasí]
a little bit of ...	pak ...	[pak ...]
half	gjysmë (f)	[ɟýsmə]

| dozen | dyzinë (f) | [dyzínə] |
| piece (item) | copë (f) | [tsópə] |

| size | madhësi (f) | [maðəsí] |
| scale (map ~) | shkallë (f) | [ʃkáɫə] |

minimal (adj)	minimale	[minimálɛ]
the smallest (adj)	më i vogli	[mə i vógli]
medium (adj)	i mesëm	[i mésəm]
maximal (adj)	maksimale	[maksimálɛ]
the largest (adj)	më i madhi	[mə i máði]

23. Containers

canning jar (glass ~)	kavanoz (m)	[kavanóz]
tin, can	kanoçe (f)	[kanótʃɛ]
bucket	kovë (f)	[kóvə]
barrel	fuçi (f)	[futʃí]
wash basin (e.g., plastic ~)	legen (m)	[lɛgén]
tank (100L water ~)	tank (m)	[tank]
hip flask	faqore (f)	[facórɛ]
jerrycan	bidon (m)	[bidón]
tank (e.g., tank car)	cisternë (f)	[tsistérnə]
mug	tas (m)	[tas]
cup (of coffee, etc.)	filxhan (m)	[fildʒán]
saucer	pjatë filxhani (f)	[pjátə fildʒáni]
glass (tumbler)	gotë (f)	[gótə]
wine glass	gotë vere (f)	[gótə vérɛ]
stock pot (soup pot)	tenxhere (f)	[tɛndʒérɛ]
bottle (~ of wine)	shishe (f)	[ʃíʃɛ]
neck (of the bottle, etc.)	grykë	[grýkə]
carafe (decanter)	brokë (f)	[brókə]
pitcher	shtambë (f)	[ʃtámbə]
vessel (container)	enë (f)	[énə]
pot (crock, stoneware ~)	enë (f)	[énə]
vase	vazo (f)	[vázo]
flacon, bottle (perfume ~)	shishe (f)	[ʃíʃɛ]
vial, small bottle	shishkë (f)	[ʃíʃkə]
tube (of toothpaste)	tubet (f)	[tubét]
sack (bag)	thes (m)	[θɛs]
bag (paper ~, plastic ~)	qese (f)	[césɛ]
packet (of cigarettes, etc.)	paketë (f)	[pakétə]
box (e.g. shoebox)	kuti (f)	[kutí]
crate	arkë (f)	[árkə]
basket	shportë (f)	[ʃpórtə]

HUMAN BEING

Human being. The body

24. Head

head	**kokë** (f)	[kókə]
face	**fytyrë** (f)	[fytýrə]
nose	**hundë** (f)	[húndə]
mouth	**gojë** (f)	[gójə]
eye	**sy** (m)	[sy]
eyes	**sytë**	[sýtə]
pupil	**bebëz** (f)	[bébəz]
eyebrow	**vetull** (f)	[vétuɫ]
eyelash	**qerpik** (m)	[cɛrpík]
eyelid	**qepallë** (f)	[cɛpáɫə]
tongue	**gjuhë** (f)	[ɟúhə]
tooth	**dhëmb** (m)	[ðəmb]
lips	**buzë** (f)	[búzə]
cheekbones	**mollëza** (f)	[móɫəza]
gum	**mishrat e dhëmbëve**	[míʃrat ɛ ðəmbəvɛ]
palate	**qiellzë** (f)	[ciéɫzə]
nostrils	**vrimat e hundës** (pl)	[vrímat ɛ húndəs]
chin	**mjekër** (f)	[mjékər]
jaw	**nofull** (f)	[nófuɫ]
cheek	**faqe** (f)	[fácɛ]
forehead	**ball** (m)	[báɫ]
temple	**tëmth** (m)	[təmθ]
ear	**vesh** (m)	[vɛʃ]
back of the head	**zverk** (m)	[zvɛrk]
neck	**qafë** (f)	[cáfə]
throat	**fyt** (m)	[fyt]
hair	**flokë** (pl)	[flókə]
hairstyle	**model flokësh** (m)	[modél flókəʃ]
haircut	**prerje flokësh** (f)	[prérjɛ flókəʃ]
wig	**paruke** (f)	[parúkɛ]
moustache	**mustaqe** (f)	[mustácɛ]
beard	**mjekër** (f)	[mjékər]
to have (a beard, etc.)	**lë mjekër**	[lə mjékər]
plait	**gërshet** (m)	[gərʃét]
sideboards	**baseta** (f)	[baséta]
red-haired (adj)	**flokëkuqe**	[flokəkúcɛ]
grey (hair) ·	**thinja**	[θíɲa]

| bald (adj) | qeros | [cɛrós] |
| bald patch | tullë (f) | [tútə] |

| ponytail | bishtalec (m) | [biʃtaléts] |
| fringe | balluke (f) | [batúkɛ] |

25. Human body

| hand | dorë (f) | [dórə] |
| arm | krah (m) | [krah] |

finger	gisht i dorës (m)	[gíʃt i dórəs]
toe	gisht i këmbës (m)	[gíʃt i kémbəs]
thumb	gishti i madh (m)	[gíʃti i máð]
little finger	gishti i vogël (m)	[gíʃti i vógəl]
nail	thua (f)	[θúa]

fist	grusht (m)	[grúʃt]
palm	pëllëmbë dore (f)	[pətémbə dórɛ]
wrist	kyç (m)	[kytʃ]
forearm	parakrah (m)	[parakráh]
elbow	bërryl (m)	[bərýl]
shoulder	shpatull (f)	[ʃpátut]

leg	këmbë (f)	[kémbə]
foot	shputë (f)	[ʃpútə]
knee	gju (m)	[ɟú]
calf	pulpë (f)	[púlpə]
hip	ijë (f)	[íjə]
heel	thembër (f)	[θémbər]

body	trup (m)	[trup]
stomach	stomak (m)	[stomák]
chest	kraharor (m)	[kraharór]
breast	gjoks (m)	[ɟóks]
flank	krah (m)	[krah]
back	kurriz (m)	[kuríz]
lower back	fundshpina (f)	[fundʃpína]
waist	beli (m)	[béli]

navel (belly button)	kërthizë (f)	[kərθízə]
buttocks	vithe (f)	[víθɛ]
bottom	prapanica (f)	[prapanítsa]

beauty spot	nishan (m)	[niʃán]
birthmark (café au lait spot)	shenjë lindjeje (f)	[ʃéɲə líndjɛjɛ]
tattoo	tatuazh (m)	[tatuáʒ]
scar	shenjë (f)	[ʃéɲə]

Clothing & Accessories

26. Outerwear. Coats

clothes	**rroba** (f)	[róba]
outerwear	**veshje e sipërme** (f)	[véʃjɛ ɛ sípərmɛ]
winter clothing	**veshje dimri** (f)	[véʃjɛ dímri]
coat (overcoat)	**pallto** (f)	[páɫto]
fur coat	**gëzof** (m)	[gəzóf]
fur jacket	**xhaketë lëkure** (f)	[dʒakétə ləkúrɛ]
down coat	**xhup** (m)	[dʒup]
jacket (e.g. leather ~)	**xhaketë** (f)	[dʒakétə]
raincoat (trenchcoat, etc.)	**pardesy** (f)	[pardɛsý]
waterproof (adj)	**kundër shiut**	[kúndər ʃíut]

27. Men's & women's clothing

shirt (button shirt)	**këmishë** (f)	[kəmíʃə]
trousers	**pantallona** (f)	[pantaɫóna]
jeans	**xhinse** (f)	[dʒínsɛ]
suit jacket	**xhaketë kostumi** (f)	[dʒakétə kostúmi]
suit	**kostum** (m)	[kostúm]
dress (frock)	**fustan** (m)	[fustán]
skirt	**fund** (m)	[fund]
blouse	**bluzë** (f)	[blúzə]
knitted jacket (cardigan, etc.)	**xhaketë me thurje** (f)	[dʒakétə mɛ θúrjɛ]
jacket (of a woman's suit)	**xhaketë femrash** (f)	[dʒakétə fémraʃ]
T-shirt	**bluzë** (f)	[blúzə]
shorts (short trousers)	**pantallona të shkurtra** (f)	[pantaɫóna tə ʃkúrtra]
tracksuit	**tuta sportive** (f)	[túta sportívɛ]
bathrobe	**peshqir trupi** (m)	[pɛʃcír trúpi]
pyjamas	**pizhame** (f)	[piʒámɛ]
jumper (sweater)	**triko** (f)	[tríko]
pullover	**pulovër** (m)	[pulóvər]
waistcoat	**jelek** (m)	[jɛlék]
tailcoat	**frak** (m)	[frak]
dinner suit	**smoking** (m)	[smokíŋ]
uniform	**uniformë** (f)	[unifórmə]
workwear	**rroba pune** (f)	[róba púnɛ]
boiler suit	**kominoshe** (f)	[kominóʃɛ]
coat (e.g. doctor's smock)	**uniformë** (f)	[unifórmə]

28. Clothing. Underwear

underwear	të brendshme (f)	[tə bréndʃmɛ]
pants	boksera (f)	[bokséra]
panties	brekë (f)	[brékə]
vest (singlet)	fanellë (f)	[fanétə]
socks	çorape (pl)	[tʃorápɛ]
nightdress	këmishë nate (f)	[kəmíʃə nátɛ]
bra	sytjena (f)	[sytjéna]
knee highs (knee-high socks)	çorape déri tek gjuri (pl)	[tʃorápɛ déri ték ɟúri]
tights	geta (f)	[géta]
stockings (hold ups)	çorape të holla (pl)	[tʃorápɛ tə hóɫa]
swimsuit, bikini	rrobë banje (f)	[róbə báɲɛ]

29. Headwear

hat	kapelë (f)	[kapélə]
trilby hat	kapelë republike (f)	[kapélə rɛpublíkɛ]
baseball cap	kapelë bejsbolli (f)	[kapélə bɛjsbóti]
flatcap	kapelë e sheshtë (f)	[kapélə ɛ ʃéʃtə]
beret	beretë (f)	[bɛrétə]
hood	kapuç (m)	[kapútʃ]
panama hat	kapelë panama (f)	[kapélə panamá]
knit cap (knitted hat)	kapuç leshi (m)	[kapútʃ léʃi]
headscarf	shami (f)	[ʃamí]
women's hat	kapelë femrash (f)	[kapélə fémraʃ]
hard hat	helmetë (f)	[hɛlmétə]
forage cap	kapelë ushtrie (f)	[kapélə uʃtríɛ]
helmet	helmetë (f)	[hɛlmétə]
bowler	kapelë derby (f)	[kapélə dérby]
top hat	kapelë cilindër (f)	[kapélə tsilíndər]

30. Footwear

footwear	këpucë (pl)	[kəpútsə]
shoes (men's shoes)	këpucë burrash (pl)	[kəpútsə búraʃ]
shoes (women's shoes)	këpucë grash (pl)	[kəpútsə gráʃ]
boots (e.g., cowboy ~)	çizme (pl)	[tʃízmɛ]
carpet slippers	pantofla (pl)	[pantófla]
trainers	atlete tenisi (pl)	[atlétɛ tɛnísi]
trainers	atlete (pl)	[atlétɛ]
sandals	sandale (pl)	[sandálɛ]
cobbler (shoe repairer)	këpucëtar (m)	[kəputsətár]
heel	takë (f)	[tákə]

pair (of shoes)	palë (f)	[pálə]
lace (shoelace)	lidhëse këpucësh (f)	[líðəsɛ kəpútsəʃ]
to lace up (vt)	lidh këpucët	[lið kəpútsət]
shoehorn	lugë këpucësh (f)	[lúgə kəpútsəʃ]
shoe polish	bojë këpucësh (f)	[bójə kəpútsəʃ]

31. Personal accessories

gloves	doreza (pl)	[dórəza]
mittens	doreza (f)	[doréza]
scarf (muffler)	shall (m)	[ʃaɫ]

glasses	syze (f)	[sýzɛ]
frame (eyeglass ~)	skelet syzesh (m)	[skɛlét sýzɛʃ]
umbrella	çadër (f)	[tʃádər]
walking stick	bastun (m)	[bastún]
hairbrush	furçë flokësh (f)	[fúrtʃə flókəʃ]
fan	erashkë (f)	[ɛráʃkə]

tie (necktie)	kravatë (f)	[kravátə]
bow tie	papion (m)	[papión]
braces	aski (pl)	[askí]
handkerchief	shami (f)	[ʃamí]

comb	krehër (m)	[kréhər]
hair slide	kapëse flokësh (f)	[kápəsɛ flókəʃ]
hairpin	karficë (f)	[karfítsə]
buckle	tokëz (f)	[tókəz]

| belt | rrip (m) | [rip] |
| shoulder strap | rrip supi (m) | [rip súpi] |

bag (handbag)	çantë dore (f)	[tʃántə dórɛ]
handbag	çantë (f)	[tʃántə]
rucksack	çantë shpine (f)	[tʃántə ʃpínɛ]

32. Clothing. Miscellaneous

fashion	modë (f)	[módə]
in vogue (adj)	në modë	[nə módə]
fashion designer	stilist (m)	[stilíst]

collar	jakë (f)	[jákə]
pocket	xhep (m)	[dʒɛp]
pocket (as adj)	i xhepit	[i dʒépit]
sleeve	mëngë (f)	[méŋə]
hanging loop	hallkë për varje (f)	[háɫkə pər várjɛ]
flies (on trousers)	zinxhir (m)	[zindʒír]

zip (fastener)	zinxhir (m)	[zindʒír]
fastener	kapëse (f)	[kápəsɛ]
button	kopsë (f)	[kópsə]

buttonhole	vrimë kopse (f)	[vrímə kópsɛ]
to come off (ab. button)	këputet	[kəpútɛt]

to sew (vi, vt)	qep	[cɛp]
to embroider (vi, vt)	qëndis	[cəndís]
embroidery	qëndisje (f)	[cəndísjɛ]
sewing needle	gjilpërë për qepje (f)	[ɟilpə́rə pər cépjɛ]
thread	pe (m)	[pɛ]
seam	tegel (m)	[tɛgél]

to get dirty (vi)	bëhem pis	[bə́hɛm pis]
stain (mark, spot)	njollë (f)	[ɲótə]
to crease, to crumple	zhubros	[ʒubrós]
to tear, to rip (vt)	gris	[gris]
clothes moth	molë rrobash (f)	[mólə róbaʃ]

33. Personal care. Cosmetics

toothpaste	pastë dhëmbësh (f)	[pástə ðə́mbəʃ]
toothbrush	furçë dhëmbësh (f)	[fúrtʃə ðə́mbəʃ]
to clean one's teeth	laj dhëmbët	[laj ðə́mbət]

razor	brisk (m)	[brísk]
shaving cream	pastë rroje (f)	[pástə rójɛ]
to shave (vi)	rruhem	[rúhɛm]

soap	sapun (m)	[sapún]
shampoo	shampo (f)	[ʃampó]

scissors	gërshërë (f)	[gərʃérə]
nail file	limë thonjsh (f)	[límə θóɲʃ]
nail clippers	prerëse thonjsh (f)	[prérəsɛ θóɲʃ]
tweezers	piskatore vetullash (f)	[piskatórɛ vétutaʃ]

cosmetics	kozmetikë (f)	[kozmɛtíkə]
face mask	maskë fytyre (f)	[máskə fytýrɛ]
manicure	manikyr (m)	[manikýr]
to have a manicure	bëj manikyr	[bəj manikýr]
pedicure	pedikyr (m)	[pɛdikýr]

make-up bag	çantë kozmetike (f)	[tʃántə kozmɛtíkɛ]
face powder	pudër fytyre (f)	[púdər fytýrɛ]
powder compact	pudër kompakte (f)	[púdər kompáktɛ]
blusher	ruzh (m)	[ruʒ]

perfume (bottled)	parfum (m)	[parfúm]
toilet water (lotion)	parfum (m)	[parfúm]
lotion	krem (m)	[krɛm]
cologne	kolonjë (f)	[kolóɲə]

eyeshadow	rimel (m)	[rimél]
eyeliner	laps për sy (m)	[láps pər sy]
mascara	rimel (m)	[rimél]
lipstick	buzëkuq (m)	[buzəkúc]

nail polish	llak për thonj (m)	[ɫak pər θóɲ]
hair spray	llak flokësh (m)	[ɫak flókəʃ]
deodorant	deodorant (m)	[dɛodoránt]

cream	krem (m)	[krɛm]
face cream	krem për fytyrë (m)	[krɛm pər fytýrə]
hand cream	krem për duar (m)	[krɛm pər dúar]
anti-wrinkle cream	krem kundër rrudhave (m)	[krɛm kúndər rúðavɛ]
day cream	krem dite (m)	[krɛm dítɛ]
night cream	krem nate (m)	[krɛm nátɛ]
day (as adj)	dite	[dítɛ]
night (as adj)	nate	[nátɛ]

tampon	tampon (m)	[tampón]
toilet paper (toilet roll)	letër higjienike (f)	[létər hiɟiɛníkɛ]
hair dryer	tharëse flokësh (f)	[θárəsɛ flókəʃ]

34. Watches. Clocks

watch (wristwatch)	orë dore (f)	[órə dórɛ]
dial	faqe e orës (f)	[fácɛ ɛ órəs]
hand (clock, watch)	akrep (m)	[akrép]
metal bracelet	rrip metalik ore (m)	[rip mɛtalík órɛ]
watch strap	rrip ore (m)	[rip órɛ]

battery	bateri (f)	[batɛrí]
to be flat (battery)	e shkarkuar	[ɛ ʃkarkúar]
to change a battery	ndërroj baterinë	[ndərój batɛrínə]
to run fast	kalon shpejt	[kalón ʃpéjt]
to run slow	ngel prapa	[ŋɛl prápa]

wall clock	orë muri (f)	[órə múri]
hourglass	orë rëre (f)	[órə rərɛ]
sundial	orë diellore (f)	[órə diɛtórɛ]
alarm clock	orë me zile (f)	[órə mɛ zílɛ]
watchmaker	orëndreqës (m)	[orəndrécəs]
to repair (vt)	ndreq	[ndréc]

Food. Nutricion

meat	mish (m)	[miʃ]
chicken	pulë (f)	[púlə]
poussin	mish pule (m)	[miʃ púlɛ]
duck	rosë (f)	[rósə]
goose	patë (f)	[pátə]
game	gjah (m)	[ɟáh]
turkey	mish gjel deti (m)	[miʃ ɟɛl déti]

pork	mish derri (m)	[miʃ déri]
veal	mish viçi (m)	[miʃ vítʃi]
lamb	mish qengji (m)	[miʃ cénɟi]
beef	mish lope (m)	[miʃ lópɛ]
rabbit	mish lepuri (m)	[miʃ lépuri]

sausage (bologna, etc.)	salsiçe (f)	[salsítʃɛ]
vienna sausage (frankfurter)	salsiçe vjeneze (f)	[salsítʃɛ vjɛnézɛ]
bacon	proshutë (f)	[proʃútə]
ham	sallam (m)	[saɫám]
gammon	kofshë derri (f)	[kófʃə déri]

pâté	pate (f)	[paté]
liver	mëlçi (f)	[məltʃí]
mince (minced meat)	hamburger (m)	[hamburgér]
tongue	gjuhë (f)	[ɟúhə]

egg	ve (f)	[vɛ]
eggs	vezë (pl)	[vézə]
egg white	e bardhë veze (f)	[ɛ bárðə vézɛ]
egg yolk	e verdhë veze (f)	[ɛ vérðə vézɛ]

fish	peshk (m)	[pɛʃk]
seafood	fruta deti (pl)	[frúta déti]
crustaceans	krustace (pl)	[krustátsɛ]
caviar	havjar (m)	[havjár]

crab	gaforre (f)	[gafórɛ]
prawn	karkalec (m)	[karkaléts]
oyster	midhje (f)	[míðjɛ]
spiny lobster	karavidhe (f)	[karavíðɛ]
octopus	oktapod (m)	[oktapód]
squid	kallamarë (f)	[kaɫamárə]

sturgeon	bli (m)	[blí]
salmon	salmon (m)	[salmón]
halibut	shojzë e Atlantikut Verior (f)	[ʃójzə ɛ atlantíkut vɛriór]
cod	merluc (m)	[mɛrlúts]

mackerel	**skumbri** (m)	[skúmbri]
tuna	**tunë** (f)	[túnə]
eel	**ngjalë** (f)	[ɲálə]

trout	**troftë** (f)	[tróftə]
sardine	**sardele** (f)	[sardélɛ]
pike	**mlysh** (m)	[mlýʃ]
herring	**harengë** (f)	[haréŋə]

bread	**bukë** (f)	[búkə]
cheese	**djath** (m)	[djáθ]
sugar	**sheqer** (m)	[ʃɛcér]
salt	**kripë** (f)	[krípə]

rice	**oriz** (m)	[oríz]
pasta (macaroni)	**makarona** (f)	[makaróna]
noodles	**makarona petë** (f)	[makaróna pétə]

butter	**gjalp** (m)	[ɟalp]
vegetable oil	**vaj vegjetal** (m)	[vaj vɛɟɛtál]
sunflower oil	**vaj luledielli** (m)	[vaj lulɛdiéɫi]
margarine	**margarinë** (f)	[margarínə]

olives	**ullinj** (pl)	[uɫíɲ]
olive oil	**vaj ulliri** (m)	[vaj uɫíri]

milk	**qumësht** (m)	[cúməʃt]
condensed milk	**qumësht i kondensuar** (m)	[cúməʃt i kondɛnsúar]
yogurt	**kos** (m)	[kos]
soured cream	**salcë kosi** (f)	[sáltsə kosi]
cream (of milk)	**krem qumështi** (m)	[krɛm cúməʃti]

mayonnaise	**majonezë** (f)	[majonézə]
buttercream	**krem gjalpi** (m)	[krɛm ɟálpi]

groats (barley ~, etc.)	**drithëra** (pl)	[dríθəra]
flour	**miell** (m)	[míɛɫ]
tinned food	**konserva** (f)	[konsérva]

cornflakes	**kornfleiks** (m)	[kornfléiks]
honey	**mjaltë** (f)	[mjáltə]
jam	**reçel** (m)	[rɛtʃél]
chewing gum	**çamçakëz** (m)	[tʃamtʃakéz]

36. Drinks

water	**ujë** (m)	[újə]
drinking water	**ujë i pijshëm** (m)	[újə i píjʃəm]
mineral water	**ujë mineral** (m)	[újə minɛrál]

still (adj)	**ujë natyral**	[újə natyrál]
carbonated (adj)	**ujë i karbonuar**	[újə i karbonúar]
sparkling (adj)	**ujë i gazuar**	[újə i gazúar]
ice	**akull** (m)	[ákuɫ]

with ice	me akull	[mɛ ákuɫ]
non-alcoholic (adj)	jo alkoolik	[jo alkoolík]
soft drink	pije e lehtë (f)	[píjɛ ɛ léhtə]
refreshing drink	pije freskuese (f)	[píjɛ frɛskúɛsɛ]
lemonade	limonadë (f)	[limonádə]

spirits	likere (pl)	[likérɛ]
wine	verë (f)	[vérə]
white wine	verë e bardhë (f)	[vérə ɛ bárðə]
red wine	verë e kuqe (f)	[vérə ɛ kúcɛ]

liqueur	liker (m)	[likér]
champagne	shampanjë (f)	[ʃampáɲə]
vermouth	vermut (m)	[vɛrmút]

whisky	uiski (m)	[víski]
vodka	vodkë (f)	[vódkə]
gin	xhin (m)	[dʒin]
cognac	konjak (m)	[koɲák]
rum	rum (m)	[rum]

coffee	kafe (f)	[káfɛ]
black coffee	kafe e zezë (f)	[káfɛ ɛ zézə]
white coffee	kafe me qumësht (m)	[káfɛ mɛ cúməʃt]
cappuccino	kapuçino (m)	[kaputʃíno]
instant coffee	neskafe (f)	[nɛskáfɛ]

milk	qumësht (m)	[cúməʃt]
cocktail	koktej (m)	[koktéj]
milkshake	milkshake (f)	[milkʃákɛ]

juice	lëng frutash (m)	[ləŋ frútaʃ]
tomato juice	lëng domatesh (m)	[ləŋ domátɛʃ]
orange juice	lëng portokalli (m)	[ləŋ portokáɫi]
freshly squeezed juice	lëng frutash i freskët (m)	[ləŋ frútaʃ i fréskət]

beer	birrë (f)	[bírə]
lager	birrë e lehtë (f)	[bírə ɛ léhtə]
bitter	birrë e zezë (f)	[bírə ɛ zézə]

tea	çaj (m)	[tʃáj]
black tea	çaj i zi (m)	[tʃáj i zí]
green tea	çaj jeshil (m)	[tʃáj jɛʃíl]

37. Vegetables

| vegetables | perime (pl) | [pɛrímɛ] |
| greens | zarzavate (pl) | [zarzavátɛ] |

tomato	domate (f)	[domátɛ]
cucumber	kastravec (m)	[kastravéts]
carrot	karotë (f)	[karótə]
potato	patate (f)	[patátɛ]
onion	qepë (f)	[cépə]

garlic	hudhër (f)	[húðər]
cabbage	lakër (f)	[lákər]
cauliflower	lulelakër (f)	[lulɛlákər]
Brussels sprouts	lakër Brukseli (f)	[lákər brukséli]
broccoli	brokoli (m)	[brókoli]

beetroot	panxhar (m)	[pandʒár]
aubergine	patëllxhan (m)	[patəɫdʒán]
courgette	kungulleshë (m)	[kuŋuɫéʃə]
pumpkin	kungull (m)	[kúŋuɫ]
turnip	rrepë (f)	[répə]

parsley	majdanoz (m)	[majdanóz]
dill	kopër (f)	[kópər]
lettuce	sallatë jeshile (f)	[saɫátə jɛʃílɛ]
celery	selino (f)	[sɛlíno]
asparagus	asparagus (m)	[asparágus]
spinach	spinaq (m)	[spinác]

pea	bizele (f)	[bizélɛ]
beans	fasule (f)	[fasúlɛ]
maize	misër (m)	[mísər]
kidney bean	groshë (f)	[gróʃə]

sweet paper	spec (m)	[spɛts]
radish	rrepkë (f)	[répkə]
artichoke	angjinare (f)	[aɲinárɛ]

38. Fruits. Nuts

fruit	frut (m)	[frut]
apple	mollë (f)	[móɫə]
pear	dardhë (f)	[dárðə]
lemon	limon (m)	[limón]
orange	portokall (m)	[portokáɫ]
strawberry (garden ~)	luleshtrydhe (f)	[lulɛʃtrýðɛ]

tangerine	mandarinë (f)	[mandarínə]
plum	kumbull (f)	[kúmbuɫ]
peach	pjeshkë (f)	[pjéʃkə]
apricot	kajsi (f)	[kajsí]
raspberry	mjedër (f)	[mjédər]
pineapple	ananas (m)	[ananás]

banana	banane (f)	[banánɛ]
watermelon	shalqi (m)	[ʃalcí]
grape	rrush (m)	[ruʃ]
sour cherry	qershi vishnje (f)	[cɛrʃí víʃnɛ]
sweet cherry	qershi (f)	[cɛrʃí]
melon	pjepër (m)	[pjépər]

grapefruit	grejpfrut (m)	[grɛjpfrút]
avocado	avokado (f)	[avokádo]
papaya	papaja (f)	[papája]

| mango | mango (f) | [máŋo] |
| pomegranate | shegë (f) | [ʃégə] |

redcurrant	kaliboba e kuqe (f)	[kalibóba ε kúcε]
blackcurrant	kaliboba e zezë (f)	[kalibóba ε zézə]
gooseberry	kulumbri (f)	[kulumbrí]
bilberry	boronicë (f)	[boronítsə]
blackberry	manaferra (f)	[manaféra]

raisin	rrush i thatë (m)	[ruʃ i θátə]
fig	fik (m)	[fik]
date	hurmë (f)	[húrmə]

peanut	kikirik (m)	[kikirík]
almond	bajame (f)	[bajámε]
walnut	arrë (f)	[árə]
hazelnut	lajthi (f)	[lajθí]
coconut	arrë kokosi (f)	[árə kokósi]
pistachios	fëstëk (m)	[fəsték]

39. Bread. Sweets

bakers' confectionery (pastry)	ëmbëlsira (pl)	[əmbəlsíra]
bread	bukë (f)	[búkə]
biscuits	biskota (pl)	[biskóta]

chocolate (n)	çokollatë (f)	[tʃokołátə]
chocolate (as adj)	prej çokollate	[prεj tʃokołátε]
candy (wrapped)	karamele (f)	[karamélε]
cake (e.g. cupcake)	kek (m)	[kék]
cake (e.g. birthday ~)	tortë (f)	[tórtə]

| pie (e.g. apple ~) | tortë (f) | [tórtə] |
| filling (for cake, pie) | mbushje (f) | [mbúʃjε] |

jam (whole fruit jam)	reçel (m)	[rεtʃél]
marmalade	marmelatë (f)	[marmεlátə]
wafers	vafera (pl)	[vaféra]
ice-cream	akullore (f)	[akułórε]
pudding (Christmas ~)	puding (m)	[pudíŋ]

40. Cooked dishes

course, dish	pjatë (f)	[pjátə]
cuisine	kuzhinë (f)	[kuʒínə]
recipe	recetë (f)	[rεtsétə]
portion	racion (m)	[ratsión]

salad	sallatë (f)	[sałátə]
soup	supë (f)	[súpə]
clear soup (broth)	lëng mishi (m)	[ləŋ míʃi]
sandwich (bread)	sandviç (m)	[sandvítʃ]

fried eggs	vezë të skuqura (pl)	[véza ta skúcura]
hamburger (beefburger)	hamburger	[hamburgér]
beefsteak	biftek (m)	[bifték]

side dish	garniturë (f)	[garnitúra]
spaghetti	shpageti (pl)	[ʃpagéti]
mash	pure patatesh (f)	[puré patátɛʃ]
pizza	pica (f)	[pítsa]
porridge (oatmeal, etc.)	qull (m)	[cuł]
omelette	omëletë (f)	[omaléta]

boiled (e.g. ~ beef)	i zier	[i zíɛr]
smoked (adj)	i tymosur	[i tymósur]
fried (adj)	i skuqur	[i skúcur]
dried (adj)	i tharë	[i θára]
frozen (adj)	i ngrirë	[i ŋrírə]
pickled (adj)	i marinuar	[i marinúar]

sweet (sugary)	i ëmbël	[i émbal]
salty (adj)	i kripur	[i krípur]
cold (adj)	i ftohtë	[i ftóhta]
hot (adj)	i nxehtë	[i ndzéhta]
bitter (adj)	i hidhur	[i híður]
tasty (adj)	i shijshëm	[i ʃíjʃam]

to cook in boiling water	ziej	[zíɛj]
to cook (dinner)	gatuaj	[gatúaj]
to fry (vt)	skuq	[skuc]
to heat up (food)	ngroh	[ŋróh]

to salt (vt)	hedh kripë	[hɛð krípa]
to pepper (vt)	hedh piper	[hɛð pipér]
to grate (vt)	rendoj	[rɛndój]
peel (n)	lëkurë (f)	[lakúra]
to peel (vt)	qëroj	[carój]

41. Spices

salt	kripë (f)	[krípa]
salty (adj)	i kripur	[i krípur]
to salt (vt)	hedh kripë	[hɛð krípa]

black pepper	piper i zi (m)	[pipér i zi]
red pepper (milled ~)	piper i kuq (m)	[pipér i kuc]
mustard	mustardë (f)	[mustárda]
horseradish	rrepë djegëse (f)	[répa djégasɛ]

condiment	salcë (f)	[sáltsa]
spice	erëz (f)	[éraz]
sauce	salcë (f)	[sáltsa]
vinegar	uthull (f)	[úθuł]

| anise | anisetë (f) | [anisétə] |
| basil | borzilok (m) | [borzilók] |

cloves	karafil (m)	[karafíl]
ginger	xhenxhefil (m)	[dʒɛndʒɛfíl]
coriander	koriandër (m)	[koriándər]
cinnamon	kanellë (f)	[kanéɫə]

sesame	susam (m)	[susám]
bay leaf	gjeth dafine (m)	[ɟɛθ dafínɛ]
paprika	spec (m)	[spɛts]
caraway	kumin (m)	[kumín]
saffron	shafran (m)	[ʃafrán]

42. Meals

| food | ushqim (m) | [uʃcím] |
| to eat (vi, vt) | ha | [ha] |

breakfast	mëngjes (m)	[mənɟés]
to have breakfast	ha mëngjes	[ha mənɟés]
lunch	drekë (f)	[drékə]
to have lunch	ha drekë	[ha drékə]
dinner	darkë (f)	[dárkə]
to have dinner	ha darkë	[ha dárkə]

| appetite | oreks (m) | [oréks] |
| Enjoy your meal! | Të bëftë mirë! | [tə bəftə mírə!] |

to open (~ a bottle)	hap	[hap]
to spill (liquid)	derdh	[dérð]
to spill out (vi)	derdhje	[dérðjɛ]

to boil (vi)	ziej	[zíɛj]
to boil (vt)	ziej	[zíɛj]
boiled (~ water)	i zier	[i zíɛr]
to chill, cool down (vt)	ftoh	[ftoh]
to chill (vi)	ftohje	[ftóhjɛ]

| taste, flavour | shije (f) | [ʃíjɛ] |
| aftertaste | shije (f) | [ʃíjɛ] |

to slim down (lose weight)	dobësohem	[dobəsóhɛm]
diet	dietë (f)	[diétə]
vitamin	vitaminë (f)	[vitamínə]
calorie	kalori (f)	[kalorí]

| vegetarian (n) | vegjetarian (m) | [vɛɟɛtarián] |
| vegetarian (adj) | vegjetarian | [vɛɟɛtarián] |

fats (nutrient)	yndyrë (f)	[yndýrə]
proteins	proteinë (f)	[protɛínə]
carbohydrates	karbohidrat (m)	[karbohidrát]

slice (of lemon, ham)	fetë (f)	[fétə]
piece (of cake, pie)	copë (f)	[tsópə]
crumb (of bread, cake, etc.)	dromcë (f)	[drómtsə]

43. Table setting

spoon	lugë (f)	[lúgǝ]
knife	thikë (f)	[θíkǝ]
fork	pirun (m)	[pirún]

cup (e.g., coffee ~)	filxhan (m)	[fildʒán]
plate (dinner ~)	pjatë (f)	[pjátǝ]
saucer	pjatë filxhani (f)	[pjátǝ fildʒáni]
serviette	pecetë (f)	[pɛtsétǝ]
toothpick	kruajtëse dhëmbësh (f)	[krúajtǝsɛ ðǝmbǝʃ]

44. Restaurant

restaurant	restorant (m)	[rɛstoránt]
coffee bar	kafene (f)	[kafɛné]
pub, bar	pab (m), pijetore (f)	[pab], [pijɛtórɛ]
tearoom	çajtore (f)	[tʃajtórɛ]

waiter	kamerier (m)	[kamɛriér]
waitress	kameriere (f)	[kamɛriérɛ]
barman	banakier (m)	[banakiér]

menu	menu (f)	[mɛnú]
wine list	menu verërash (f)	[mɛnú vérǝraʃ]
to book a table	rezervoj një tavolinë	[rɛzɛrvój ɲǝ tavolínǝ]

course, dish	pjatë (f)	[pjátǝ]
to order (meal)	porosis	[porosís]
to make an order	bëj porosinë	[bǝj porosínǝ]

aperitif	aperitiv (m)	[apɛritív]
starter	antipastë (f)	[antipástǝ]
dessert, pudding	ëmbëlsirë (f)	[ǝmbǝlsírǝ]

bill	faturë (f)	[fatúrǝ]
to pay the bill	paguaj faturën	[pagúaj fatúrǝn]
to give change	jap kusur	[jap kusúr]
tip	bakshish (m)	[bakʃíʃ]

Family, relatives and friends

45. Personal information. Forms

name (first name)	emër (m)	[émər]
surname (last name)	mbiemër (m)	[mbiémər]
date of birth	datëlindje (f)	[datəlíndjɛ]
place of birth	vendlindje (f)	[vɛndlíndjɛ]
nationality	kombësi (f)	[kombəsí]
place of residence	vendbanim (m)	[vɛndbaním]
country	shtet (m)	[ʃtɛt]
profession (occupation)	profesion (m)	[profɛsión]
gender, sex	gjinia (f)	[ɟiníа]
height	gjatësia (f)	[ɟatəsía]
weight	peshë (f)	[péʃə]

46. Family members. Relatives

mother	nënë (f)	[nénə]
father	baba (f)	[babá]
son	bir (m)	[bir]
daughter	bijë (f)	[bíjə]
younger daughter	vajza e vogël (f)	[vájza ɛ vógəl]
younger son	djali i vogël (m)	[djáli i vógəl]
eldest daughter	vajza e madhe (f)	[vájza ɛ máðɛ]
eldest son	djali i vogël (m)	[djáli i vógəl]
brother	vëlla (m)	[vəɫá]
elder brother	vëllai i madh (m)	[vəɫai i mað]
younger brother	vëllai i vogël (m)	[vəɫai i vógəl]
sister	motër (f)	[mótər]
elder sister	motra e madhe (f)	[mótra ɛ máðɛ]
younger sister	motra e vogël (f)	[mótra ɛ vógəl]
cousin (masc.)	kushëri (m)	[kuʃərí]
cousin (fem.)	kushërirë (f)	[kuʃərírə]
mummy	mami (f)	[mámi]
dad, daddy	babi (m)	[bábi]
parents	prindër (pl)	[príndər]
child	fëmijë (f)	[fəmíjə]
children	fëmijë (pl)	[fəmíjə]
grandmother	gjyshe (f)	[ɟýʃɛ]
grandfather	gjysh (m)	[ɟyʃ]

grandson	nip (m)	[nip]
granddaughter	mbesë (f)	[mbésə]
grandchildren	nipër e mbesa (pl)	[nípər ɛ mbésa]

uncle	dajë (f)	[dájə]
aunt	teze (f)	[tézɛ]
nephew	nip (m)	[nip]
niece	mbesë (f)	[mbésə]

mother-in-law (wife's mother)	vjehrrë (f)	[vjéhrə]
father-in-law (husband's father)	vjehrri (m)	[vjéhri]
son-in-law (daughter's husband)	dhëndër (m)	[ðéndər]
stepmother	njerkë (f)	[ɲérkə]
stepfather	njerk (m)	[ɲérk]

infant	foshnjë (f)	[fóʃnə]
baby (infant)	fëmijë (f)	[fəmíjə]
little boy, kid	djalosh (m)	[djalóʃ]

wife	bashkëshorte (f)	[baʃkəʃórtɛ]
husband	bashkëshort (m)	[baʃkəʃórt]
spouse (husband)	bashkëshort (m)	[baʃkəʃórt]
spouse (wife)	bashkëshorte (f)	[baʃkəʃórtɛ]

married (masc.)	i martuar	[i martúar]
married (fem.)	e martuar	[ɛ martúar]
single (unmarried)	beqar	[bɛcár]
bachelor	beqar (m)	[bɛcár]
divorced (masc.)	i divorcuar	[i divortsúar]
widow	vejushë (f)	[vɛjúʃə]
widower	vejan (m)	[vɛján]

relative	kushëri (m)	[kuʃərí]
close relative	kushëri i afërt (m)	[kuʃərí i áfərt]
distant relative	kushëri i largët (m)	[kuʃərí i lárgət]
relatives	kushërinj (pl)	[kuʃəríɲ]

orphan (boy)	jetim (m)	[jɛtím]
orphan (girl)	jetime (f)	[jɛtímɛ]
guardian (of a minor)	kujdestar (m)	[kujdɛstár]
to adopt (a boy)	adoptoj	[adoptój]
to adopt (a girl)	adoptoj	[adoptój]

Medicine

47. Diseases

illness	sëmundje (f)	[səmúndjɛ]
to be ill	jam sëmurë	[jam səmúrə]
health	shëndet (m)	[ʃəndét]
runny nose (coryza)	rrifë (f)	[rífə]
tonsillitis	grykët (m)	[grýkət]
cold (illness)	ftohje (f)	[ftóhjɛ]
to catch a cold	ftohem	[ftóhɛm]
bronchitis	bronkit (m)	[bronkít]
pneumonia	pneumoni (f)	[pnɛumoní]
flu, influenza	grip (m)	[grip]
shortsighted (adj)	miop	[mióp]
longsighted (adj)	presbit	[prɛsbít]
strabismus (crossed eyes)	strabizëm (m)	[strabízəm]
squint-eyed (adj)	strabik	[strabík]
cataract	katarakt (m)	[katarákt]
glaucoma	glaukoma (f)	[glaukóma]
stroke	goditje (f)	[godítjɛ]
heart attack	sulm në zemër (m)	[sulm nə zémər]
myocardial infarction	infarkt miokardiak (m)	[infárkt miokardiák]
paralysis	paralizë (f)	[paralízə]
to paralyse (vt)	paralizoj	[paralizój]
allergy	alergji (f)	[alɛrɟí]
asthma	astmë (f)	[ástmə]
diabetes	diabet (m)	[diabét]
toothache	dhimbje dhëmbi (f)	[ðímbjɛ ðə́mbi]
caries	karies (m)	[kariés]
diarrhoea	diarre (f)	[diaré]
constipation	kapsllëk (m)	[kapsɫék]
stomach upset	dispepsi (f)	[dispɛpsí]
food poisoning	helmim (m)	[hɛlmím]
to get food poisoning	helmohem nga ushqimi	[hɛlmóhɛm ŋa uʃcími]
arthritis	artrit (m)	[artrít]
rickets	rakit (m)	[rakít]
rheumatism	reumatizëm (m)	[rɛumatízəm]
atherosclerosis	arteriosklerozë (f)	[artɛrioskɫerózə]
gastritis	gastrit (m)	[gastrít]
appendicitis	apendicit (m)	[apɛnditsít]

| cholecystitis | kolecistit (m) | [kolɛtsistít] |
| ulcer | ulcerë (f) | [ultsérə] |

measles	fruth (m)	[fruθ]
rubella (German measles)	rubeola (f)	[rubɛóla]
jaundice	verdhëza (f)	[vérðəza]
hepatitis	hepatit (m)	[hɛpatít]

schizophrenia	skizofreni (f)	[skizofrɛní]
rabies (hydrophobia)	sëmundje e tërbimit (f)	[səmúndjɛ ɛ tərbímit]
neurosis	neurozë (f)	[nɛurózə]
concussion	tronditje (f)	[trondítjɛ]

cancer	kancer (m)	[kantsér]
sclerosis	sklerozë (f)	[sklɛrózə]
multiple sclerosis	sklerozë e shumëfishtë (f)	[sklɛrózə ɛ ʃuməfíʃtə]

alcoholism	alkoolizëm (m)	[alkoolízəm]
alcoholic (n)	alkoolik (m)	[alkoolík]
syphilis	sifiliz (m)	[sifilíz]
AIDS	SIDA (f)	[sída]

tumour	tumor (m)	[tumór]
malignant (adj)	malinj	[malíɲ]
benign (adj)	beninj	[bɛníɲ]

fever	ethe (f)	[éθɛ]
malaria	malarie (f)	[malaríɛ]
gangrene	gangrenë (f)	[gaɲrénə]
seasickness	sëmundje deti (f)	[səmúndjɛ déti]
epilepsy	epilepsi (f)	[ɛpilɛpsí]

epidemic	epidemi (f)	[ɛpidɛmí]
typhus	tifo (f)	[tífo]
tuberculosis	tuberkuloz (f)	[tubɛrkulóz]
cholera	kolerë (f)	[kolérə]
plague (bubonic ~)	murtaja (f)	[murtája]

48. Symptoms. Treatments. Part 1

symptom	simptomë (f)	[simptómə]
temperature	temperaturë (f)	[tɛmpɛratúrə]
high temperature (fever)	temperaturë e lartë (f)	[tɛmpɛratúrə ɛ lártə]
pulse (heartbeat)	puls (m)	[puls]

dizziness (vertigo)	marrje mendsh (m)	[márjɛ méndʃ]
hot (adj)	i nxehtë	[i ndzéhtə]
shivering	drithërima (f)	[driθəríma]
pale (e.g. ~ face)	i zbehur	[i zbéhur]

cough	kollë (f)	[kótə]
to cough (vi)	kollitem	[kotítɛm]
to sneeze (vi)	teshtij	[tɛʃtíj]
faint	të fikët (f)	[tə fíkət]

47

to faint (vi)	bie të fikët	[bíɛ tə fíkət]
bruise (hématome)	mavijosje (f)	[mavijósjɛ]
bump (lump)	gungë (f)	[gúŋə]
to bang (bump)	godas	[godás]
contusion (bruise)	lëndim (m)	[ləndím]
to get a bruise	lëndohem	[ləndóhɛm]

to limp (vi)	çaloj	[tʃalój]
dislocation	dislokim (m)	[dislokím]
to dislocate (vt)	del nga vendi	[dɛl ŋa véndi]
fracture	thyerje (f)	[θýɛrjɛ]
to have a fracture	thyej	[θýɛj]

cut (e.g. paper ~)	e prerë (f)	[ɛ prérə]
to cut oneself	pres veten	[prɛs vétɛn]
bleeding	rrjedhje gjaku (f)	[rjéðjɛ ɉáku]

| burn (injury) | djegie (f) | [djégiɛ] |
| to get burned | digjem | [díɉɛm] |

to prick (vt)	shpoj	[ʃpoj]
to prick oneself	shpohem	[ʃpóhɛm]
to injure (vt)	dëmtoj	[dəmtój]
injury	dëmtim (m)	[dəmtím]
wound	plagë (f)	[plágə]
trauma	traumë (f)	[traúmə]

to be delirious	fol përçart	[fól pərtʃárt]
to stutter (vi)	belbëzoj	[bɛlbəzój]
sunstroke	pikë e diellit (f)	[píkə ɛ diéɫit]

49. Symptoms. Treatments. Part 2

| pain, ache | dhimbje (f) | [ðímbjɛ] |
| splinter (in foot, etc.) | cifël (f) | [tsífəl] |

sweat (perspiration)	djersë (f)	[djérsə]
to sweat (perspire)	djersij	[djɛrsíj]
vomiting	të vjella (f)	[tə vjéɫa]
convulsions	konvulsione (f)	[konvulsiónɛ]

pregnant (adj)	shtatzënë	[ʃtatzénə]
to be born	lind	[lind]
delivery, labour	lindje (f)	[líndjɛ]
to deliver (~ a baby)	sjell në jetë	[sjɛɫ nə jétə]
abortion	abort (m)	[abórt]

breathing, respiration	frymëmarrje (f)	[fryməmárjɛ]
in-breath (inhalation)	mbajtje e frymës (f)	[mbájtjɛ ɛ frýməs]
out-breath (exhalation)	lëshim i frymës (m)	[ləʃím i frýməs]
to exhale (breathe out)	nxjerr frymën	[ndzjér frýmən]
to inhale (vi)	marr frymë	[mar frýmə]
disabled person	invalid (m)	[invalíd]
cripple	i gjymtuar (m)	[i ɉymtúar]

drug addict	narkoman (m)	[narkomán]
deaf (adj)	shurdh	[ʃurð]
mute (adj)	memec	[mɛméts]
deaf mute (adj)	shurdh-memec	[ʃurð-mɛméts]

mad, insane (adj)	i marrë	[i márə]
madman (demented person)	i çmendur (m)	[i tʃméndur]
madwoman	e çmendur (f)	[ɛ tʃméndur]
to go insane	çmendem	[tʃméndɛm]

gene	gen (m)	[gɛn]
immunity	imunitet (m)	[imunitét]
hereditary (adj)	e trashëguar	[ɛ traʃəgúar]
congenital (adj)	e lindur	[ɛ líndur]

virus	virus (m)	[virús]
microbe	mikrob (m)	[mikrób]
bacterium	bakterie (f)	[baktériɛ]
infection	infeksion (m)	[infɛksión]

50. Symptoms. Treatments. Part 3

| hospital | spital (m) | [spitál] |
| patient | pacient (m) | [patsiént] |

diagnosis	diagnozë (f)	[diagnózə]
cure	kurë (f)	[kúrə]
medical treatment	trajtim mjekësor (m)	[trajtím mjɛkəsór]
to get treatment	kurohem	[kuróhɛm]
to treat (~ a patient)	kuroj	[kurój]
to nurse (look after)	kujdesem	[kujdésɛm]
care (nursing ~)	kujdes (m)	[kujdés]

operation, surgery	operacion (m)	[opɛratsión]
to bandage (head, limb)	fashoj	[faʃój]
bandaging	fashim (m)	[faʃím]

vaccination	vaksinim (m)	[vaksiním]
to vaccinate (vt)	vaksinoj	[vaksinój]
injection	injeksion (m)	[iɲɛksión]
to give an injection	bëj injeksion	[bəj iɲɛksíon]

attack	atak (m)	[aták]
amputation	amputim (m)	[amputím]
to amputate (vt)	amputoj	[amputój]
coma	komë (f)	[kómə]
to be in a coma	jam në komë	[jam nə kómə]
intensive care	kujdes intensiv (m)	[kujdés intɛnsív]

to recover (~ from flu)	shërohem	[ʃəróhɛm]
condition (patient's ~)	gjendje (f)	[ɟéndjɛ]
consciousness	vetëdije (f)	[vɛtədíjɛ]
memory (faculty)	kujtesë (f)	[kujtésə]

to pull out (tooth)	heq	[hɛc]
filling	mbushje (f)	[mbúʃjɛ]
to fill (a tooth)	mbush	[mbúʃ]

hypnosis	hipnozë (f)	[hipnózə]
to hypnotize (vt)	hipnotizim	[hipnotizím]

51. Doctors

doctor	mjek (m)	[mjék]
nurse	infermiere (f)	[infɛrmiérɛ]
personal doctor	mjek personal (m)	[mjék pɛrsonál]

dentist	dentist (m)	[dɛntíst]
optician	okulist (m)	[okulíst]
general practitioner	mjek i përgjithshëm (m)	[mjék i pərɲíθʃəm]
surgeon	kirurg (m)	[kirúrg]

psychiatrist	psikiatër (m)	[psikiátər]
paediatrician	pediatër (m)	[pɛdiátər]
psychologist	psikolog (m)	[psikológ]
gynaecologist	gjinekolog (m)	[ɟinɛkológ]
cardiologist	kardiolog (m)	[kardiológ]

52. Medicine. Drugs. Accessories

medicine, drug	ilaç (m)	[ilátʃ]
remedy	mjekim (m)	[mjɛkím]
to prescribe (vt)	shkruaj recetë	[ʃkrúaj rɛtsétə]
prescription	recetë (f)	[rɛtsétə]

tablet, pill	pilulë (f)	[pilúlə]
ointment	krem (m)	[krɛm]
ampoule	ampulë (f)	[ampúlə]
mixture, solution	përzierje (f)	[pərzíɛrjɛ]
syrup	shurup (m)	[ʃurúp]
capsule	pilulë (f)	[pilúlə]
powder	pudër (f)	[púdər]

gauze bandage	fashë garze (f)	[faʃə gárzɛ]
cotton wool	pambuk (m)	[pambúk]
iodine	jod (m)	[jod]

plaster	leukoplast (m)	[lɛukoplást]
eyedropper	pikatore (f)	[pikatórɛ]
thermometer	termometër (m)	[tɛrmométər]
syringe	shiringë (f)	[ʃiríŋə]

wheelchair	karrocë me rrota (f)	[karótsə mɛ róta]
crutches	paterica (f)	[patɛrítsa]
painkiller	qetësues (m)	[cɛtəsúɛs]
laxative	laksativ (m)	[laksatív]

spirits (ethanol)	**alkool dezinfektues** (m)	[alkoól dɛzinfɛktúɛs]
medicinal herbs	**bimë mjekësore** (f)	[bímə mjɛkəsórɛ]
herbal (~ tea)	**çaj bimor**	[tʃáj bimór]

HUMAN HABITAT

City

city, town	qytet (m)	[cytét]
capital city	kryeqytet (m)	[kryɛcytét]
village	fshat (m)	[ffát]
city map	hartë e qytetit (f)	[hártə ɛ cytétit]
city centre	qendër e qytetit (f)	[céndər ɛ cytétit]
suburb	periferi (f)	[pɛrifɛrí]
suburban (adj)	periferik	[pɛrifɛrík]
outskirts	periferia (f)	[pɛrifɛría]
environs (suburbs)	periferia (f)	[pɛrifɛría]
city block	bllok pallatesh (m)	[bɫók paɫátɛʃ]
residential block (area)	bllok banimi (m)	[bɫók baními]
traffic	trafik (m)	[trafík]
traffic lights	semafor (m)	[sɛmafór]
public transport	transport publik (m)	[transpórt publík]
crossroads	kryqëzim (m)	[krycəzím]
zebra crossing	kalim për këmbësorë (m)	[kalím pər kəmbəsórə]
pedestrian subway	nënkalim për këmbësorë (m)	[nənkalím pər kəmbəsórə]
to cross (~ the street)	kapërcej	[kapərtséj]
pedestrian	këmbësor (m)	[kəmbəsór]
pavement	trotuar (m)	[trotuár]
bridge	urë (f)	[úrə]
embankment (river walk)	breg lumi (m)	[brɛg lúmi]
fountain	shatërvan (m)	[ʃatərván]
allée (garden walkway)	rrugëz (m)	[rúgəz]
park	park (m)	[park]
boulevard	bulevard (m)	[bulɛvárd]
square	shesh (m)	[ʃɛʃ]
avenue (wide street)	bulevard (m)	[bulɛvárd]
street	rrugë (f)	[rúgə]
side street	rrugë dytësore (f)	[rúgə dytəsórɛ]
dead end	rrugë pa krye (f)	[rúgə pa krýɛ]
house	shtëpi (f)	[ʃtəpí]
building	ndërtesë (f)	[ndərtésə]
skyscraper	qiellgërvishtës (m)	[ciɛɫgərvíʃtəs]
facade	fasadë (f)	[fasádə]
roof	çati (f)	[tʃatí]

window	dritare (f)	[dritárɛ]
arch	hark (m)	[hárk]
column	kolonë (f)	[kolónə]
corner	kënd (m)	[kə́nd]

shop window	vitrinë (f)	[vitrínə]
signboard (store sign, etc.)	tabelë (f)	[tabélə]
poster (e.g., playbill)	poster (m)	[postér]
advertising poster	afishe reklamuese (f)	[afíʃɛ rɛklamúɛsɛ]
hoarding	tabelë reklamash (f)	[tabélə rɛklámaʃ]

rubbish	plehra (f)	[pléhra]
rubbish bin	kosh plehrash (m)	[koʃ pléhraʃ]
to litter (vi)	hedh mbeturina	[hɛð mbɛturína]
rubbish dump	deponi plehrash (f)	[dɛponí pléhraʃ]

telephone box	kabinë telefonike (f)	[kabínə tɛlɛfoníkɛ]
lamppost	shtyllë dritash (f)	[ʃtýłə drítaʃ]
bench (park ~)	stol (m)	[stol]

police officer	polic (m)	[políts]
police	polici (f)	[politsí]
beggar	lypës (m)	[lýpəs]
homeless (n)	i pastrehë (m)	[i pastréhə]

54. Urban institutions

shop	dyqan (m)	[dycán]
chemist, pharmacy	farmaci (f)	[farmatsí]
optician (spectacles shop)	optikë (f)	[optíkə]
shopping centre	qendër tregtare (f)	[céndər trɛgtárɛ]
supermarket	supermarket (m)	[supɛrmarkét]

bakery	furrë (f)	[fúrə]
baker	furrtar (m)	[furtár]
cake shop	pastiçeri (f)	[pastitʃɛrí]
grocery shop	dyqan ushqimor (m)	[dycán uʃcimór]
butcher shop	dyqan mishi (m)	[dycán míʃi]

| greengrocer | dyqan fruta-perimesh (m) | [dycán frúta-pɛrímɛʃ] |
| market | treg (m) | [trɛg] |

coffee bar	kafene (f)	[kafɛné]
restaurant	restorant (m)	[rɛstoránt]
pub, bar	pab (m), pijetore (f)	[pab], [pijɛtórɛ]
pizzeria	piceri (f)	[pitsɛrí]

hairdresser	parukeri (f)	[parukɛrí]
post office	zyrë postare (f)	[zýrə postárɛ]
dry cleaners	pastrim kimik (m)	[pastrím kimík]
photo studio	studio fotografike (f)	[stúdio fotografíkɛ]

| shoe shop | dyqan këpucësh (m) | [dycán kəpútsəʃ] |
| bookshop | librari (f) | [librarí] |

sports shop	dyqan me mallra sportivë (m)	[dycán mɛ mátra sportívə]
clothes repair shop	rrobaqepësi (f)	[robacɛpəsí]
formal wear hire	dyqan veshjesh me qira (m)	[dycán véʃjɛʃ mɛ cirá]
video rental shop	dyqan videosh me qira (m)	[dycán vídɛoʃ mɛ cirá]

circus	cirk (m)	[tsírk]
zoo	kopsht zoologjik (m)	[kópʃt zooloɟík]
cinema	kinema (f)	[kinɛmá]
museum	muze (m)	[muzé]
library	bibliotekë (f)	[bibliotékə]

theatre	teatër (m)	[tɛátər]
opera (opera house)	opera (f)	[opéra]
nightclub	klub nate (m)	[klúb nátɛ]
casino	kazino (f)	[kazíno]

mosque	xhami (f)	[dʒamí]
synagogue	sinagogë (f)	[sinagógə]
cathedral	katedrale (f)	[katɛdrálɛ]
temple	tempull (m)	[témpuɫ]
church	kishë (f)	[kíʃə]

college	kolegj (m)	[koléɟ]
university	universitet (m)	[univɛrsitét]
school	shkollë (f)	[ʃkóɫə]

prefecture	prefekturë (f)	[prɛfɛktúrə]
town hall	bashki (f)	[baʃkí]
hotel	hotel (m)	[hotél]
bank	bankë (f)	[bánkə]

embassy	ambasadë (f)	[ambasádə]
travel agency	agjenci udhëtimesh (f)	[aɟɛntsí uðətímɛʃ]
information office	zyrë informacioni (f)	[zýrə informatsióni]
currency exchange	këmbim valutor (m)	[kəmbím valutór]

| underground, tube | metro (f) | [mɛtró] |
| hospital | spital (m) | [spitál] |

| petrol station | pikë karburanti (f) | [píkə karburánti] |
| car park | parking (m) | [parkíŋ] |

55. Signs

signboard (store sign, etc.)	tabelë (f)	[tabélə]
notice (door sign, etc.)	njoftim (m)	[ɲoftím]
poster	poster (m)	[postér]
direction sign	tabelë drejtuese (f)	[tabélə drɛjtúɛsɛ]
arrow (sign)	shigjetë (f)	[ʃiɟétə]

caution	kujdes (m)	[kujdés]
warning sign	shenjë paralajmëruese (f)	[ʃéɲə paralajmərúɛsɛ]
to warn (vt)	paralajmëroj	[paralajmərój]

rest day (weekly ~)	ditë pushimi (f)	[dítə puʃími]
timetable (schedule)	orar (m)	[orár]
opening hours	orari i punës (m)	[orári i púnəs]

WELCOME!	MIRË SE VINI!	[mírə sɛ víni!]
ENTRANCE	HYRJE	[hýrjɛ]
WAY OUT	DALJE	[dáljɛ]

PUSH	SHTY	[ʃty]
PULL	TËRHIQ	[tərhíc]
OPEN	HAPUR	[hápur]
CLOSED	MBYLLUR	[mbýɫur]

| WOMEN | GRA | [gra] |
| MEN | BURRA | [búra] |

DISCOUNTS	ZBRITJE	[zbrítjɛ]
SALE	ULJE	[úljɛ]
NEW!	TË REJA!	[tə réja!]
FREE	FALAS	[fálas]

ATTENTION!	KUJDES!	[kujdés!]
NO VACANCIES	NUK KA VENDE TË LIRA	[nuk ka véndɛ tə líra]
RESERVED	E REZERVUAR	[ɛ rɛzɛrvúar]

| ADMINISTRATION | ADMINISTRATA | [administráta] |
| STAFF ONLY | VETËM PËR STAFIN | [vétəm pər stáfin] |

BEWARE OF THE DOG!	RUHUNI NGA QENI!	[rúhuni ŋa céni!]
NO SMOKING	NDALOHET DUHANI	[ndalóhɛt duháni]
DO NOT TOUCH!	MOS PREK!	[mos prék!]

DANGEROUS	TË RREZIKSHME	[tə rɛzíkʃmɛ]
DANGER	RREZIK	[rɛzík]
HIGH VOLTAGE	TENSION I LARTË	[tɛnsión i lártə]
NO SWIMMING!	NUK LEJOHET NOTI!	[nuk lɛjóhɛt nóti!]
OUT OF ORDER	E PRISHUR	[ɛ príʃur]

FLAMMABLE	LËNDË DJEGËSE	[ləndə djégəsɛ]
FORBIDDEN	E NDALUAR	[ɛ ndalúar]
NO TRESPASSING!	NDALOHET HYRJA	[ndalóhɛt hýrja]
WET PAINT	BOJË E FRESKËT	[bójə ɛ fréskət]

56. Urban transport

bus, coach	autobus (m)	[autobús]
tram	tramvaj (m)	[tramváj]
trolleybus	autobus tramvaj (m)	[autobús tramváj]
route (bus ~)	itinerar (m)	[itinɛrár]
number (e.g. bus ~)	numër (m)	[númər]

to go by ...	udhëtoj me ...	[uðətój mɛ ...]
to get on (~ the bus)	hip	[hip]
to get off ...	zbres ...	[zbrɛs ...]

stop (e.g. bus ~)	stacion (m)	[statsión]
next stop	stacioni tjetër (m)	[statsióni tjétər]
terminus	terminal (m)	[tɛrminál]
timetable	orar (m)	[orár]
to wait (vt)	pres	[prɛs]

| ticket | biletë (f) | [bilétə] |
| fare | çmim bilete (m) | [tʃmím bilétɛ] |

cashier (ticket seller)	shitës biletash (m)	[ʃítəs bilétaʃ]
ticket inspection	kontroll biletash (m)	[kontróɫ bilétaʃ]
ticket inspector	kontrollues biletash (m)	[kontroɫúɛs bilétaʃ]

to be late (for ...)	vonohem	[vonóhɛm]
to miss (~ the train, etc.)	humbas	[humbás]
to be in a hurry	nxitoj	[ndzitój]

taxi, cab	taksi (m)	[táksi]
taxi driver	shofer taksie (m)	[ʃofér taksíɛ]
by taxi	me taksi	[mɛ táksi]
taxi rank	stacion taksish (m)	[statsión táksiʃ]
to call a taxi	thërras taksi	[θərás táksi]
to take a taxi	marr taksi	[mar táksi]

traffic	trafik (m)	[trafík]
traffic jam	bllokim trafiku (m)	[bɫokím trafíku]
rush hour	orë e trafikut të rëndë (f)	[órə ɛ trafíkut tə rəndə]
to park (vi)	parkoj	[parkój]
to park (vt)	parkim	[parkím]
car park	parking (m)	[parkíŋ]

underground, tube	metro (f)	[mɛtró]
station	stacion (m)	[statsión]
to take the tube	shkoj me metro	[ʃkoj mɛ métro]
train	tren (m)	[trɛn]
train station	stacion treni (m)	[statsión tréni]

57. Sightseeing

monument	monument (m)	[monumént]
fortress	kala (f)	[kalá]
palace	pallat (m)	[paɫát]
castle	kështjellë (f)	[kəʃtjétə]
tower	kullë (f)	[kúɫə]
mausoleum	mauzoleum (m)	[mauzolɛúm]

architecture	arkitekturë (f)	[arkitɛktúrə]
medieval (adj)	mesjetare	[mɛsjɛtárɛ]
ancient (adj)	e lashtë	[ɛ láʃtə]
national (adj)	kombëtare	[kombətárɛ]
famous (monument, etc.)	i famshëm	[i fámʃəm]

| tourist | turist (m) | [turíst] |
| guide (person) | udhërrëfyes (m) | [uðərəfýɛs] |

excursion, sightseeing tour	ekskursion (m)	[ɛkskursión]
to show (vt)	tregoj	[trɛgój]
to tell (vt)	dëftoj	[dəftój]

to find (vt)	gjej	[ɟéj]
to get lost (lose one's way)	humbas	[humbás]
map (e.g. underground ~)	hartë (f)	[hártə]
map (e.g. city ~)	hartë (f)	[hártə]

souvenir, gift	suvenir (m)	[suvɛnír]
gift shop	dyqan dhuratash (m)	[dycán ðurátaʃ]
to take pictures	bëj foto	[bəj fóto]
to have one's picture taken	bëj fotografi	[bəj fotografí]

58. Shopping

to buy (purchase)	blej	[blɛj]
shopping	blerje (f)	[blérjɛ]
to go shopping	shkoj për pazar	[ʃkoj pər pazár]
shopping	pazar (m)	[pazár]

| to be open (ab. shop) | hapur | [hápur] |
| to be closed | mbyllur | [mbýɫur] |

footwear, shoes	këpucë (f)	[kəpútsə]
clothes, clothing	veshje (f)	[véʃjɛ]
cosmetics	kozmetikë (f)	[kozmɛtíkə]
food products	mallra ushqimore (f)	[máɫra uʃcimórɛ]
gift, present	dhuratë (f)	[ðurátə]

| shop assistant (masc.) | shitës (m) | [ʃítəs] |
| shop assistant (fem.) | shitëse (f) | [ʃítəsɛ] |

cash desk	arkë (f)	[árkə]
mirror	pasqyrë (f)	[pascýrə]
counter (shop ~)	banak (m)	[bának]
fitting room	dhomë prove (f)	[ðómə próvɛ]

to try on	provoj	[provój]
to fit (ab. dress, etc.)	më rri mirë	[mə ri mírə]
to fancy (vt)	pëlqej	[pəlcéj]

price	çmim (m)	[tʃmím]
price tag	etiketa e çmimit (f)	[ɛtikéta ɛ tʃmímit]
to cost (vt)	kushton	[kuʃtón]
How much?	Sa?	[sa?]
discount	ulje (f)	[úljɛ]

inexpensive (adj)	jo e shtrenjtë	[jo ɛ ʃtréɲtə]
cheap (adj)	e lirë	[ɛ lírə]
expensive (adj)	i shtrenjtë	[i ʃtréɲtə]
It's expensive	Është e shtrenjtë	[əʃtə ɛ ʃtréɲtə]
hire (n)	qiramarrje (f)	[ciramárjɛ]
to hire (~ a dinner jacket)	marr me qira	[mar mɛ cirá]

| credit (trade credit) | kredit (m) | [krɛdít] |
| on credit (adv) | me kredi | [mɛ krɛdí] |

59. Money

money	para (f)	[pará]
currency exchange	këmbim valutor (m)	[kəmbím valutór]
exchange rate	kurs këmbimi (m)	[kurs kəmbími]
cashpoint	bankomat (m)	[bankomát]
coin	monedhë (f)	[monéðə]

| dollar | dollar (m) | [doɫár] |
| euro | euro (f) | [éuro] |

lira	lirë (f)	[lírə]
Deutschmark	Marka gjermane (f)	[márka ɟɛrmánɛ]
franc	franga (f)	[fráŋa]
pound sterling	sterlina angleze (f)	[stɛrlína aŋlézɛ]
yen	jen (m)	[jén]

debt	borxh (m)	[bórdʒ]
debtor	debitor (m)	[dɛbitór]
to lend (money)	jap hua	[jap huá]
to borrow (vi, vt)	marr hua	[mar huá]

bank	bankë (f)	[bánkə]
account	llogari (f)	[ɫogarí]
to deposit (vt)	depozitoj	[dɛpozitój]
to deposit into the account	depozitoj në llogari	[dɛpozitój nə ɫogarí]
to withdraw (vt)	tërheq	[tərhéc]

credit card	kartë krediti (f)	[kártə krɛdíti]
cash	kesh (m)	[kɛʃ]
cheque	çek (m)	[tʃék]
to write a cheque	lëshoj një çek	[ləʃój ɲə tʃék]
chequebook	bllok çeqesh (m)	[bɫók tʃécɛʃ]

wallet	portofol (m)	[portofól]
purse	kuletë (f)	[kulétə]
safe	kasafortë (f)	[kasafórtə]

heir	trashëgimtar (m)	[traʃəgimtár]
inheritance	trashëgimi (f)	[traʃəgimí]
fortune (wealth)	pasuri (f)	[pasurí]

lease	qira (f)	[cirá]
rent (money)	qiraja (f)	[cirája]
to rent (sth from sb)	marr me qira	[mar mɛ cirá]

price	çmim (m)	[tʃmím]
cost	kosto (f)	[kósto]
sum	shumë (f)	[ʃúmə]
to spend (vt)	shpenzoj	[ʃpɛnzój]
expenses	shpenzime (f)	[ʃpɛnzímɛ]

| to economize (vi, vt) | kursej | [kurséj] |
| economical | ekonomik | [εkonomík] |

to pay (vi, vt)	paguaj	[pagúaj]
payment	pagesë (f)	[pagésə]
change (give the ~)	kusur (m)	[kusúr]

tax	taksë (f)	[táksə]
fine	gjobë (f)	[ɟóbə]
to fine (vt)	vendos gjobë	[vεndós ɟóbə]

60. Post. Postal service

post office	zyrë postare (f)	[zýrə postárε]
post (letters, etc.)	postë (f)	[póstə]
postman	postier (m)	[postiér]
opening hours	orari i punës (m)	[orári i púnəs]

letter	letër (f)	[létər]
registered letter	letër rekomande (f)	[létər rεkomándε]
postcard	kartolinë (f)	[kartolínə]
telegram	telegram (m)	[tεlεgrám]
parcel	pako (f)	[páko]
money transfer	transfer parash (m)	[transfér paráʃ]

to receive (vt)	pranoj	[pranój]
to send (vt)	dërgoj	[dərgój]
sending	dërgesë (f)	[dərgésə]

address	adresë (f)	[adrésə]
postcode	kodi postar (m)	[kódi postár]
sender	dërguesi (m)	[dərgúεsi]
receiver	pranues (m)	[pranúεs]

| name (first name) | emër (m) | [émər] |
| surname (last name) | mbiemër (m) | [mbiémər] |

postage rate	tarifë postare (f)	[tarífə postárε]
standard (adj)	standard	[standárd]
economical (adj)	ekonomike	[εkonomíkε]

weight	peshë (f)	[péʃə]
to weigh (~ letters)	peshoj	[pεʃój]
envelope	zarf (m)	[zarf]
postage stamp	pullë postare (f)	[púłə postárε]
to stamp an envelope	vendos pullën postare	[vεndós púłən postárε]

Dwelling. House. Home

61. House. Electricity

electricity	**elektricitet** (m)	[ɛlɛktritsitét]
light bulb	**poç** (m)	[potʃ]
switch	**çelës drite** (m)	[tʃéləs drítɛ]
fuse (plug fuse)	**siguresë** (f)	[sigurésə]
cable, wire (electric ~)	**kabllo** (f)	[kábɫo]
wiring	**rrjet elektrik** (m)	[rjét ɛlɛktrík]
electricity meter	**njehsor elektrik** (m)	[ɲɛhsór ɛlɛktrík]
readings	**matjet** (pl)	[mátjɛt]

62. Villa. Mansion

country house	**vilë** (f)	[vílə]
country-villa	**vilë** (f)	[vílə]
wing (~ of a building)	**krah** (m)	[krah]
garden	**kopsht** (m)	[kopʃt]
park	**park** (m)	[park]
conservatory (greenhouse)	**serrë** (f)	[sérə]
to look after (garden, etc.)	**përkujdesem**	[pərkujdésɛm]
swimming pool	**pishinë** (f)	[piʃínə]
gym (home gym)	**palestër** (f)	[paléstər]
tennis court	**fushë tenisi** (f)	[fúʃə tɛnísi]
home theater (room)	**sallon teatri** (m)	[saɫón tɛátri]
garage	**garazh** (m)	[garáʒ]
private property	**pronë private** (f)	[prónə privátɛ]
private land	**tokë private** (f)	[tókə privátɛ]
warning (caution)	**paralajmërim** (m)	[paralajmərím]
warning sign	**shenjë paralajmëruese** (f)	[ʃéɲə paralajmərúɛsɛ]
security	**sigurim** (m)	[sigurím]
security guard	**roje sigurimi** (m)	[rójɛ sigurími]
burglar alarm	**alarm** (m)	[alárm]

63. Flat

flat	**apartament** (m)	[apartamént]
room	**dhomë** (f)	[ðómə]
bedroom	**dhomë gjumi** (f)	[ðómə ɟúmi]

dining room	dhomë ngrënie (f)	[ðómə ŋrəníɛ]
living room	dhomë ndeje (f)	[ðómə ndéjɛ]
study (home office)	dhomë pune (f)	[ðómə púnɛ]

entry room	hyrje (f)	[hýrjɛ]
bathroom	banjo (f)	[báɲo]
water closet	tualet (m)	[tualét]

ceiling	tavan (m)	[taván]
floor	dysheme (f)	[dyʃɛmé]
corner	qoshe (f)	[cóʃɛ]

64. Furniture. Interior

furniture	orendi (f)	[orɛndí]
table	tryezë (f)	[tryézə]
chair	karrige (f)	[karígɛ]
bed	shtrat (m)	[ʃtrat]

| sofa, settee | divan (m) | [diván] |
| armchair | kolltuk (m) | [koɫtúk] |

| bookcase | raft librash (m) | [ráft líbraʃ] |
| shelf | sergjen (m) | [sɛrɟén] |

wardrobe	gardërobë (f)	[gardəróbə]
coat rack (wall-mounted ~)	varëse (f)	[várəsɛ]
coat stand	varëse xhaketash (f)	[várəsɛ dʒakétaʃ]

| chest of drawers | komodë (f) | [komódə] |
| coffee table | tryezë e ulët (f) | [tryéza ɛ úlət] |

mirror	pasqyrë (f)	[pascýrə]
carpet	qilim (m)	[cilím]
small carpet	tapet (m)	[tapét]

fireplace	oxhak (m)	[odʒák]
candle	qiri (m)	[círi]
candlestick	shandan (m)	[ʃandán]

drapes	perde (f)	[pérdɛ]
wallpaper	tapiceri (f)	[tapitsɛrí]
blinds (jalousie)	grila (f)	[gríla]

| table lamp | llambë tavoline (f) | [ɫámbə tavolínɛ] |
| wall lamp (sconce) | llambadar muri (m) | [ɫambadár múri] |

| standard lamp | llambadar (m) | [ɫambadár] |
| chandelier | llambadar (m) | [ɫambadár] |

leg (of a chair, table)	këmbë (f)	[kémbə]
armrest	mbështetëse krahu (f)	[mbəʃtétəsɛ kráhu]
back (backrest)	mbështetëse (f)	[mbəʃtétəsɛ]
drawer	sirtar (m)	[sirtár]

65. Bedding

bedclothes	çarçafë (pl)	[tʃartʃáfə]
pillow	jastëk (m)	[jasték]
pillowslip	këllëf jastëku (m)	[kəłəf jastéku]
duvet	jorgan (m)	[jorgán]
sheet	çarçaf (m)	[tʃartʃáf]
bedspread	mbulesë (f)	[mbulésə]

66. Kitchen

kitchen	kuzhinë (f)	[kuʒínə]
gas	gaz (m)	[gaz]
gas cooker	sobë me gaz (f)	[sóbə mɛ gaz]
electric cooker	sobë elektrike (f)	[sóbə ɛlɛktríkɛ]
oven	furrë (f)	[fúrə]
microwave oven	mikrovalë (f)	[mikroválə]
refrigerator	frigorifer (m)	[frigorifér]
freezer	frigorifer (m)	[frigorifér]
dishwasher	pjatalarëse (f)	[pjatalárəsɛ]
mincer	grirëse mishi (f)	[grírəsɛ míʃi]
juicer	shtrydhëse frutash (f)	[ʃtrýðəsɛ frútaʃ]
toaster	toster (m)	[tostér]
mixer	mikser (m)	[miksér]
coffee machine	makinë kafeje (f)	[makínə kaféjɛ]
coffee pot	kafetierë (f)	[kafɛtiérə]
coffee grinder	mulli kafeje (f)	[mułí káfɛjɛ]
kettle	çajnik (m)	[tʃajník]
teapot	çajnik (m)	[tʃajník]
lid	kapak (m)	[kapák]
tea strainer	sitë çaji (f)	[sítə tʃáji]
spoon	lugë (f)	[lúgə]
teaspoon	lugë çaji (f)	[lúgə tʃáji]
soup spoon	lugë gjelle (f)	[lúgə ɟéłɛ]
fork	pirun (m)	[pirún]
knife	thikë (f)	[θíkə]
tableware (dishes)	enë kuzhine (f)	[énə kuʒínɛ]
plate (dinner ~)	pjatë (f)	[pjátə]
saucer	pjatë filxhani (f)	[pjátə fildʒáni]
shot glass	potir (m)	[potír]
glass (tumbler)	gotë (f)	[gótə]
cup	filxhan (m)	[fildʒán]
sugar bowl	tas për sheqer (m)	[tas pər ʃɛcér]
salt cellar	kripore (f)	[kripórɛ]
pepper pot	enë piperi (f)	[énə pipéri]

butter dish	**pjatë gjalpi** (f)	[pjátə ɟálpi]
stock pot (soup pot)	**tenxhere** (f)	[tɛndʒérɛ]
frying pan (skillet)	**tigan** (m)	[tigán]
ladle	**garuzhdë** (f)	[garúʒdə]
colander	**kullesë** (f)	[kułésə]
tray (serving ~)	**tabaka** (f)	[tabaká]

bottle	**shishe** (f)	[ʃíʃɛ]
jar (glass)	**kavanoz** (m)	[kavanóz]
tin (can)	**kanoçe** (f)	[kanótʃɛ]

bottle opener	**hapëse shishesh** (f)	[hapəsé ʃíʃɛʃ]
tin opener	**hapëse kanoçesh** (f)	[hapəsé kanótʃɛʃ]
corkscrew	**turjelë tapash** (f)	[turjélə tápaʃ]
filter	**filtër** (m)	[fíltər]
to filter (vt)	**filtroj**	[filtrój]

waste (food ~, etc.)	**pleh** (m)	[plɛh]
waste bin (kitchen ~)	**kosh plehrash** (m)	[koʃ pléhraʃ]

67. Bathroom

bathroom	**banjo** (f)	[báɲo]
water	**ujë** (m)	[újə]
tap	**rubinet** (m)	[rubinét]
hot water	**ujë i nxehtë** (f)	[újə i ndzéhtə]
cold water	**ujë i ftohtë** (f)	[újə i ftóhtə]

toothpaste	**pastë dhëmbësh** (f)	[pástə ðémbəʃ]
to clean one's teeth	**laj dhëmbët**	[laj ðémbət]
toothbrush	**furçë dhëmbësh** (f)	[fúrtʃə ðémbəʃ]

to shave (vi)	**rruhem**	[rúhɛm]
shaving foam	**shkumë rroje** (f)	[ʃkumə rójɛ]
razor	**brisk** (m)	[brísk]

to wash (one's hands, etc.)	**laj duart**	[laj dúart]
to have a bath	**lahem**	[láhɛm]
shower	**dush** (m)	[duʃ]
to have a shower	**bëj dush**	[bəj dúʃ]

bath	**vaskë** (f)	[váskə]
toilet (toilet bowl)	**tualet** (m)	[tualét]
sink (washbasin)	**lavaman** (m)	[lavamán]

soap	**sapun** (m)	[sapún]
soap dish	**pjatë sapuni** (f)	[pjátə sapúni]

sponge	**sfungjer** (m)	[sfunɟér]
shampoo	**shampo** (f)	[ʃampó]
towel	**peshqir** (m)	[pɛʃcír]
bathrobe	**peshqir trupi** (m)	[pɛʃcír trúpi]
laundry (laundering)	**larje** (f)	[lárjɛ]
washing machine	**makinë larëse** (f)	[makínə lárəsɛ]

| to do the laundry | laj rroba | [laj róba] |
| washing powder | detergjent (m) | [dɛtɛrjént] |

68. Household appliances

TV, telly	televizor (m)	[tɛlɛvizór]
tape recorder	inçizues me shirit (m)	[intʃizúɛs mɛ ʃirít]
video	video regjistrues (m)	[vídɛo rɛʝistrúɛs]
radio	radio (f)	[rádio]
player (CD, MP3, etc.)	kasetofon (m)	[kasɛtofón]

video projector	projektor (m)	[projɛktór]
home cinema	kinema shtëpie (f)	[kinɛmá ʃtəpíɛ]
DVD player	DVD player (m)	[dividí plɛjər]
amplifier	amplifikator (m)	[amplifikatór]
video game console	konsol video loje (m)	[konsól vídɛo lójɛ]

video camera	videokamerë (f)	[vidɛokamérə]
camera (photo)	aparat fotografik (m)	[aparát fotografík]
digital camera	kamerë digjitale (f)	[kamérə diʝitálɛ]

vacuum cleaner	fshesë elektrike (f)	[fʃésə ɛlɛktríkɛ]
iron (e.g. steam ~)	hekur (m)	[hékur]
ironing board	tryezë për hekurosje (f)	[tryézə pər hɛkurósjɛ]

telephone	telefon (m)	[tɛlɛfón]
mobile phone	celular (m)	[tsɛlulár]
typewriter	makinë shkrimi (f)	[makínə ʃkrími]
sewing machine	makinë qepëse (f)	[makínə cépəsɛ]

microphone	mikrofon (m)	[mikrofón]
headphones	kufje (f)	[kúfjɛ]
remote control (TV)	telekomandë (f)	[tɛlɛkomándə]

CD, compact disc	CD (f)	[tsɛdé]
cassette, tape	kasetë (f)	[kasétə]
vinyl record	pllakë gramafoni (f)	[płákə gramafóni]

HUMAN ACTIVITIES

Job. Business. Part 1

office (company ~)	zyrë (f)	[zýrə]
office (director's ~)	zyrë (f)	[zýrə]
reception desk	recepsion (m)	[rɛtsɛpsión]
secretary	sekretar (m)	[sɛkrɛtár]
secretary (fem.)	sekretare (f)	[sɛkrɛtárɛ]
director	drejtor (m)	[drɛjtór]
manager	menaxher (m)	[mɛnadʒér]
accountant	kontabilist (m)	[kontabilíst]
employee	punonjës (m)	[punóɲəs]
furniture	orendi (f)	[orɛndí]
desk	tavolinë pune (f)	[tavolínə púnɛ]
desk chair	karrige pune (f)	[karígɛ púnɛ]
drawer unit	njësi sirtarësh (f)	[ɲəsí sirtárəʃ]
coat stand	varëse xhaketash (f)	[várəsɛ dʒakétaʃ]
computer	kompjuter (m)	[kompjutér]
printer	printer (m)	[printér]
fax machine	aparat faksi (m)	[aparát fáksi]
photocopier	fotokopje (f)	[fotokópjɛ]
paper	letër (f)	[létər]
office supplies	pajisje zyre (f)	[pajísjɛ zýrɛ]
mouse mat	shtroje e mausit (f)	[ʃtrójɛ ɛ máusit]
sheet of paper	fletë (f)	[flétə]
binder	dosje (f)	[dósjɛ]
catalogue	katalog (m)	[katalóg]
phone directory	numerator telefonik (m)	[numɛratór tɛlɛfoník]
documentation	dokumentacion (m)	[dokumɛntatsión]
brochure (e.g. 12 pages ~)	broshurë (f)	[broʃúrə]
leaflet (promotional ~)	fletëpalosje (f)	[flɛtəpalósjɛ]
sample	mostër (f)	[móstər]
training meeting	takim trajnimi (m)	[takím trajními]
meeting (of managers)	takim (m)	[takím]
lunch time	pushim dreke (m)	[puʃím drékɛ]
to make a copy	bëj fotokopje	[bəj fotokópjɛ]
to make multiple copies	shumëfishoj	[ʃuməfiʃój]
to receive a fax	marr faks	[mar fáks]
to send a fax	dërgoj faks	[dərgój fáks]

to call (by phone)	telefonoj	[tɛlɛfonój]
to answer (vt)	përgjigjem	[pəɟíɟɛm]
to put through	kaloj linjën	[kalój líɲən]

to arrange, to set up	lë takim	[lə takím]
to demonstrate (vt)	tregoj	[trɛgój]
to be absent	mungoj	[muɲój]
absence	mungesë (f)	[muɲésə]

70. Business processes. Part 1

business	biznes (m)	[biznés]
occupation	profesion (m)	[profɛsión]

firm	firmë (f)	[fírmə]
company	kompani (f)	[kompaní]
corporation	korporatë (f)	[korporátə]
enterprise	ndërmarrje (f)	[ndərmárjɛ]
agency	agjenci (f)	[aɟɛntsí]

agreement (contract)	marrëveshje (f)	[marəvéʃɛ]
contract	kontratë (f)	[kontrátə]
deal	marrëveshje (f)	[marəvéʃɛ]
order (to place an ~)	porosi (f)	[porosí]
terms (of the contract)	kushte (f)	[kúʃtɛ]

wholesale (adv)	me shumicë	[mɛ ʃumítsə]
wholesale (adj)	me shumicë	[mɛ ʃumítsə]
wholesale (n)	me shumicë (f)	[mɛ ʃumítsə]
retail (adj)	me pakicë	[mɛ pakítsə]
retail (n)	me pakicë (f)	[mɛ pakítsə]

competitor	konkurrent (m)	[konkurént]
competition	konkurrencë (f)	[konkuréntsə]
to compete (vi)	konkurroj	[konkurój]

partner (associate)	ortak (m)	[orták]
partnership	partneritet (m)	[partnɛritét]

crisis	krizë (f)	[krízə]
bankruptcy	falimentim (m)	[falimɛntím]
to go bankrupt	falimentoj	[falimɛntój]
difficulty	vështirësi (f)	[vəʃtirəsí]
problem	problem (m)	[problém]
catastrophe	katastrofë (f)	[katastrófə]

economy	ekonomi (f)	[ɛkonomí]
economic (~ growth)	ekonomik	[ɛkonomík]
economic recession	recesion ekonomik (m)	[rɛtsɛsión ɛkonomík]

goal (aim)	qëllim (m)	[cəɬím]
task	detyrë (f)	[dɛtýrə]
to trade (vi)	tregtoj	[trɛgtój]
network (distribution ~)	rrjet (m)	[rjét]

| inventory (stock) | inventar (m) | [invɛntár] |
| range (assortment) | gamë (f) | [gámə] |

leader (leading company)	lider (m)	[lidér]
large (~ company)	e madhe	[ɛ máðɛ]
monopoly	monopol (m)	[monopól]

theory	teori (f)	[tɛorí]
practice	praktikë (f)	[praktíkə]
experience (in my ~)	përvojë (f)	[pərvójə]
trend (tendency)	trend (m)	[trɛnd]
development	zhvillim (m)	[ʒviɫím]

71. Business processes. Part 2

| profit (foregone ~) | fitim (m) | [fitím] |
| profitable (~ deal) | fitimprurës | [fitimprúrəs] |

delegation (group)	delegacion (m)	[dɛlɛgatsión]
salary	pagë (f)	[págə]
to correct (an error)	korrigjoj	[koriɟój]
business trip	udhëtim pune (m)	[uðətím púnɛ]
commission	komision (m)	[komisión]

to control (vt)	kontrolloj	[kontroɫój]
conference	konferencë (f)	[konfɛréntsə]
licence	licencë (f)	[litséntsə]
reliable (~ partner)	i besueshëm	[i bɛsúɛʃem]

initiative (undertaking)	nismë (f)	[nísmə]
norm (standard)	normë (f)	[nórmə]
circumstance	rrethanë (f)	[rɛθánə]
duty (of an employee)	detyrë (f)	[dɛtýrə]

organization (company)	organizatë (f)	[organizátə]
organization (process)	organizativ (m)	[organizatív]
organized (adj)	i organizuar	[i organizúar]
cancellation	anulim (m)	[anulím]
to cancel (call off)	anuloj	[anulój]
report (official ~)	raport (m)	[rapórt]

patent	patentë (f)	[paténtə]
to patent (obtain patent)	patentoj	[patɛntój]
to plan (vt)	planifikoj	[planifikój]

bonus (money)	bonus (m)	[bonús]
professional (adj)	profesional	[profɛsionál]
procedure	procedurë (f)	[protsɛdúrə]

to examine (contract, etc.)	shqyrtoj	[ʃcyrtój]
calculation	llogaritje (f)	[ɫogarítjɛ]
reputation	reputacion (m)	[rɛputatsión]
risk	rrezik (m)	[rɛzík]
to manage, to run	drejtoj	[drɛjtój]

information (report)	informacion (m)	[informatsión]
property	pronë (f)	[prónə]
union	bashkim (m)	[baʃkím]

life insurance	sigurim jete (m)	[sigurím jétɛ]
to insure (vt)	siguroj	[sigurój]
insurance	sigurim (m)	[sigurím]

auction (~ sale)	ankand (m)	[ankánd]
to notify (inform)	njoftoj	[ɲoftój]
management (process)	menaxhim (m)	[mɛnadʒím]
service (~ industry)	shërbim (m)	[ʃərbím]

forum	forum (m)	[forúm]
to function (vi)	funksionoj	[funksionój]
stage (phase)	fazë (f)	[fázə]
legal (~ services)	ligjor	[liɟór]
lawyer (legal advisor)	avokat (m)	[avokát]

72. Production. Works

plant	uzinë (f)	[uzínə]
factory	fabrikë (f)	[fabríkə]
workshop	punëtori (f)	[punətorí]
works, production site	punishte (f)	[puníʃtɛ]

industry (manufacturing)	industri (f)	[industrí]
industrial (adj)	industrial	[industriál]
heavy industry	industri e rëndë (f)	[industrí ɛ rəndə]
light industry	industri e lehtë (f)	[industrí ɛ léhtə]

products	produkt (m)	[prodúkt]
to produce (vt)	prodhoj	[proðój]
raw materials	lëndë e parë (f)	[léndə ɛ párə]

foreman (construction ~)	përgjegjës (m)	[pərɟéɟəs]
workers team (crew)	skuadër (f)	[skuádər]
worker	punëtor (m)	[punətór]

working day	ditë pune (f)	[dítə púnɛ]
pause (rest break)	pushim (m)	[puʃím]
meeting	mbledhje (f)	[mbléðjɛ]
to discuss (vt)	diskutoj	[diskutój]

plan	plan (m)	[plan]
to fulfil the plan	përmbush planin	[pərmbúʃ plánin]
rate of output	normë prodhimi (f)	[nórmə proðími]
quality	cilësi (f)	[tsiləsí]
control (checking)	kontroll (m)	[kontróɫ]
quality control	kontroll cilësie (m)	[kontróɫ tsiləsíɛ]

workplace safety	siguri në punë (f)	[sigurí nə púnə]
discipline	disiplinë (f)	[disiplínə]
violation (of safety rules, etc.)	thyerje rregullash (f)	[θýɛrjɛ réguɫaʃ]

to violate (rules)	thyej rregullat	[θýɛj réguɫat]
strike	grevë (f)	[grévə]
striker	grevist (m)	[grɛvíst]
to be on strike	jam në grevë	[jam nə grévə]
trade union	sindikatë punëtorësh (f)	[sindikátə punətórəʃ]

to invent (machine, etc.)	shpik	[ʃpik]
invention	shpikje (f)	[ʃpíkjɛ]
research	kërkim (m)	[kərkím]
to improve (make better)	përmirësoj	[pərmirəsój]
technology	teknologji (f)	[tɛknoloʝí]
technical drawing	vizatim teknik (m)	[vizatím tɛkník]

load, cargo	ngarkesë (f)	[ŋarkésə]
loader (person)	ngarkues (m)	[ŋarkúɛs]
to load (vehicle, etc.)	ngarkoj	[ŋarkój]
loading (process)	ngarkimi	[ŋarkími]
to unload (vi, vt)	shkarkoj	[ʃkarkój]
unloading	shkarkim (m)	[ʃkarkím]

transport	transport (m)	[transpórt]
transport company	agjenci transporti (f)	[aʝɛntsí transpórti]
to transport (vt)	transportoj	[transportój]

wagon	vagon mallrash (m)	[vagón máɫraʃ]
tank (e.g., oil ~)	cisternë (f)	[tsistérnə]
lorry	kamion (m)	[kamión]

| machine tool | makineri veglash (f) | [makinɛrí vɛgláʃ] |
| mechanism | mekanizëm (m) | [mɛkanízəm] |

industrial waste	mbetje industriale (f)	[mbétjɛ industriálɛ]
packing (process)	paketim (m)	[pakɛtím]
to pack (vt)	paketoj	[pakɛtój]

73. Contract. Agreement

contract	kontratë (f)	[kontrátə]
agreement	marrëveshje (f)	[marəvéʃɛ]
addendum	shtojcë (f)	[ʃtójtsə]

to sign a contract	nënshkruaj një kontratë	[nənʃkrúaj ɲə kontrátə]
signature	nënshkrim (m)	[nənʃkrím]
to sign (vt)	nënshkruaj	[nənʃkrúaj]
seal (stamp)	vulë (f)	[vúlə]

subject of the contract	objekt i kontratës (m)	[objékt i kontrátəs]
clause	kusht (m)	[kuʃt]
parties (in contract)	palët (m)	[pálət]
legal address	adresa zyrtare (f)	[adrésa zyrtárɛ]

to violate the contract	mosrespektim kontrate	[mosrɛspɛktím kontrátɛ]
commitment (obligation)	detyrim (m)	[dɛtyrím]
responsibility	përgjegjësi (f)	[pərɟɛɟəsí]

force majeure	forcë madhore (f)	[fórtsə maðórɛ]
dispute	mosmarrëveshje (f)	[mosmarəvéʃjɛ]
penalties	ndëshkime (pl)	[ndəʃkímɛ]

74. Import & Export

import	import (m)	[impórt]
importer	importues (m)	[importúɛs]
to import (vt)	importoj	[importój]
import (as adj.)	i importuar	[i importúar]

export (exportation)	eksport (m)	[ɛksport]
exporter	eksportues (m)	[ɛksportúɛs]
to export (vt)	eksportoj	[ɛksportój]
export (as adj.)	i eksportuar	[i ɛksportúar]

| goods (merchandise) | mallra (pl) | [máɬra] |
| consignment, lot | ngarkesë (f) | [ŋarkésə] |

weight	peshë (f)	[péʃə]
volume	vëllim (m)	[vəɬím]
cubic metre	metër kub (m)	[métər kúb]

manufacturer	prodhues (m)	[proðúɛs]
transport company	agjenci transporti (f)	[aɟɛntsí transpórti]
container	kontejner (m)	[kontɛjnér]

border	kufi (m)	[kufí]
customs	doganë (f)	[dogánə]
customs duty	taksë doganore (f)	[táksə doganórɛ]
customs officer	doganier (m)	[doganiér]
smuggling	trafikim (m)	[trafikím]
contraband (smuggled goods)	kontrabandë (f)	[kontrabándə]

75. Finances

share, stock	stok (m)	[stok]
bond (certificate)	certifikatë valutore (f)	[tsɛrtifikátə valutórɛ]
promissory note	letër me vlerë (f)	[létər mɛ vlérə]

| stock exchange | bursë (f) | [búrsə] |
| stock price | çmimi i stokut (m) | [tʃmími i stókut] |

| to go down (become cheaper) | ulet | [úlɛt] |
| to go up (become more expensive) | rritet | [rítɛt] |

share	kuotë (f)	[kuótə]
controlling interest	përqindje kontrolluese (f)	[pərcíndjɛ kontroɬúɛsɛ]
investment	investim (m)	[invɛstím]

to invest (vt)	investoj	[invɛstój]
percent	përqindje (f)	[pərcíndjɛ]
interest (on investment)	interes (m)	[intɛrés]

profit	fitim (m)	[fitím]
profitable (adj)	fitimprurës	[fitimprúrəs]
tax	taksë (f)	[táksə]

currency (foreign ~)	valutë (f)	[valútə]
national (adj)	kombëtare	[kombətárɛ]
exchange (currency ~)	këmbim valute (m)	[kəmbím valútɛ]

| accountant | kontabilist (m) | [kontabilíst] |
| accounting | kontabilitet (m) | [kontabilitét] |

bankruptcy	falimentim (m)	[falimɛntím]
collapse, ruin	kolaps (m)	[koláps]
ruin	rrënim (m)	[rəním]
to be ruined (financially)	rrënohem	[rənóhɛm]
inflation	inflacion (m)	[inflatsión]
devaluation	zhvlerësim (m)	[ʒvlɛrəsím]

capital	kapital (m)	[kapitál]
income	të ardhura (f)	[tə árðura]
turnover	qarkullim (m)	[carkuɫím]
resources	burime (f)	[burímɛ]
monetary resources	burime monetare (f)	[burímɛ monɛtárɛ]

| overheads | shpenzime bazë (f) | [ʃpɛnzímɛ bázə] |
| to reduce (expenses) | zvogëloj | [zvogəlój] |

76. Marketing

marketing	marketing (m)	[markɛtíŋ]
market	treg (m)	[trɛg]
market segment	segment tregu (m)	[sɛgmént trégu]
product	produkt (m)	[prodúkt]
goods (merchandise)	mallra (pl)	[máɫra]

brand	markë (f)	[márkə]
trademark	markë tregtare (f)	[márkə trɛgtárɛ]
logotype	logo (f)	[lógo]
logo	logo (f)	[lógo]

demand	kërkesë (f)	[kərkésə]
supply	furnizim (m)	[furnizím]
need	nevojë (f)	[nɛvójə]
consumer	konsumator (m)	[konsumatór]

analysis	analizë (f)	[analízə]
to analyse (vt)	analizoj	[analizój]
positioning	vendosje (f)	[vɛndósjɛ]
to position (vt)	vendos	[vɛndós]
price	çmim (m)	[tʃmím]

| pricing policy | politikë e çmimeve (f) | [politíkǝ ɛ tʃmímɛvɛ] |
| price formation | formim i çmimit (m) | [formím i tʃmímit] |

77. Advertising

advertising	reklamë (f)	[rɛklámǝ]
to advertise (vt)	reklamoj	[rɛklamój]
budget	buxhet (m)	[budʒét]

ad, advertisement	reklamë (f)	[rɛklámǝ]
TV advertising	reklamë televizive (f)	[rɛklámǝ tɛlɛvizívɛ]
radio advertising	reklamë në radio (f)	[rɛklámǝ nǝ rádio]
outdoor advertising	reklamë ambientale (f)	[rɛklámǝ ambiɛntálɛ]

mass medias	masmedia (f)	[masmédia]
periodical (n)	botim periodik (m)	[botím pɛriodík]
image (public appearance)	imazh (m)	[imáʒ]

| slogan | slogan (m) | [slogán] |
| motto (maxim) | moto (f) | [móto] |

campaign	fushatë (f)	[fuʃátǝ]
advertising campaign	fushatë reklamuese (f)	[fuʃátǝ rɛklamúɛsɛ]
target group	grup i synuar (m)	[grup i synúar]

business card	kartëvizitë (f)	[kartǝvizítǝ]
leaflet (promotional ~)	fletëpalosje (f)	[flɛtǝpalósjɛ]
brochure (e.g. 12 pages ~)	broshurë (f)	[broʃúrǝ]
pamphlet	pamflet (m)	[pamflét]
newsletter	buletin (m)	[bulɛtín]

signboard (store sign, etc.)	tabelë (f)	[tabélǝ]
poster	poster (m)	[postér]
hoarding	tabelë reklamash (f)	[tabélǝ rɛklámaʃ]

78. Banking

| bank | bankë (f) | [bánkǝ] |
| branch (of a bank) | degë (f) | [dégǝ] |

| consultant | punonjës banke (m) | [punóɲǝs bánkɛ] |
| manager (director) | drejtor (m) | [drɛjtór] |

bank account	llogari bankare (f)	[ɫogarí bankárɛ]
account number	numër llogarie (m)	[númǝr ɫogaríɛ]
current account	llogari rrjedhëse (f)	[ɫogarí rjéðǝsɛ]
deposit account	llogari kursimesh (f)	[ɫogarí kursímɛʃ]

to open an account	hap një llogari	[hap ɲǝ ɫogarí]
to close the account	mbyll një llogari	[mbýɫ ɲǝ ɫogarí]
to deposit into the account	depozitoj në llogari	[dɛpozitój nǝ ɫogarí]
to withdraw (vt)	tërheq	[tǝrhéc]

deposit	depozitë (f)	[dɛpozítə]
to make a deposit	kryej një depozitim	[krýɛj ɲə dɛpozitím]
wire transfer	transfer bankar (m)	[transfér bankár]
to wire, to transfer	transferoj para	[transfɛrój pará]

| sum | shumë (f) | [ʃúmə] |
| How much? | Sa? | [sa?] |

| signature | nënshkrim (m) | [nənʃkrím] |
| to sign (vt) | nënshkruaj | [nənʃkrúaj] |

credit card	kartë krediti (f)	[kártə krɛdíti]
code (PIN code)	kodi PIN (m)	[kódi pin]
credit card number	numri i kartës së kreditit (m)	[númri i kártəs sə krɛdítit]
cashpoint	bankomat (m)	[bankomát]

cheque	çek (m)	[tʃɛk]
to write a cheque	lëshoj një çek	[ləʃój ɲə tʃék]
chequebook	bllok çeqesh (m)	[bɫók tʃécɛʃ]

loan (bank ~)	kredi (f)	[krɛdí]
to apply for a loan	aplikoj për kredi	[aplikój pər krɛdí]
to get a loan	marr kredi	[mar krɛdí]
to give a loan	jap kredi	[jap krɛdí]
guarantee	garanci (f)	[garantsí]

79. Telephone. Phone conversation

telephone	telefon (m)	[tɛlɛfón]
mobile phone	celular (m)	[tsɛlulár]
answerphone	sekretari telefonike (f)	[sɛkrɛtarí tɛlɛfoníkɛ]

| to call (by phone) | telefonoj | [tɛlɛfonój] |
| call, ring | telefonatë (f) | [tɛlɛfonátə] |

to dial a number	i bie numrit	[i bíɛ númrit]
Hello!	Përshëndetje!	[pərʃəndétjɛ!]
to ask (vt)	pyes	[pýɛs]
to answer (vi, vt)	përgjigjem	[pərɟíɟɛm]

to hear (vt)	dëgjoj	[dəɟój]
well (adv)	mirë	[mírə]
not well (adv)	jo mirë	[jo mírə]
noises (interference)	zhurmë (f)	[ʒúrmə]

receiver	marrës (m)	[márəs]
to pick up (~ the phone)	ngre telefonin	[ŋré tɛlɛfónin]
to hang up (~ the phone)	mbyll telefonin	[mbýɫ tɛlɛfónin]

busy (engaged)	i zënë	[i zénə]
to ring (ab. phone)	bie zilja	[bíɛ zílja]
telephone book	numerator telefonik (m)	[numɛratór tɛlɛfoník]
local (adj)	lokale	[lokálɛ]
local call	thirrje lokale (f)	[θírjɛ lokálɛ]

trunk (e.g. ~ call)	distancë e largët	[distántsə ε lárgət]
trunk call	thirrje në distancë (f)	[θírjε nə distántsə]
international (adj)	ndërkombëtar	[ndərkombətár]
international call	thirrje ndërkombëtare (f)	[θírjε ndərkombətárε]

80. Mobile telephone

mobile phone	celular (m)	[tsεlulár]
display	ekran (m)	[εkrán]
button	buton (m)	[butón]
SIM card	karta SIM (m)	[kárta sim]
battery	bateri (f)	[batεrí]
to be flat (battery)	e shkarkuar	[ε ʃkarkúar]
charger	karikues (m)	[karikúεs]
menu	menu (f)	[mεnú]
settings	parametra (f)	[paramétra]
tune (melody)	melodi (f)	[mεlodí]
to select (vt)	përzgjedh	[pərzʝéð]
calculator	makinë llogaritëse (f)	[makínə ɫogarítəsε]
voice mail	postë zanore (f)	[póstə zanórε]
alarm clock	alarm (m)	[alárm]
contacts	kontakte (pl)	[kontáktε]
SMS (text message)	SMS (m)	[εsεmεs]
subscriber	abonent (m)	[abonént]

81. Stationery

ballpoint pen	stilolaps (m)	[stiloláps]
fountain pen	stilograf (m)	[stilográf]
pencil	laps (m)	[láps]
highlighter	shënjues (m)	[ʃəɲúεs]
felt-tip pen	tushë me bojë (f)	[túʃə mε bójə]
notepad	bllok shënimesh (m)	[bɫók ʃənímεʃ]
diary	agjendë (f)	[aʝéndə]
ruler	vizore (f)	[vizórε]
calculator	makinë llogaritëse (f)	[makínə ɫogarítəsε]
rubber	gomë (f)	[gómə]
drawing pin	pineskë (f)	[pinéskə]
paper clip	kapëse fletësh (f)	[kápεsε flétəʃ]
glue	ngjitës (m)	[nʝítəs]
stapler	ngjitës metalik (m)	[nʝítəs mεtalík]
hole punch	hapës vrimash (m)	[hápəs vrímaʃ]
pencil sharpener	mprehëse lapsash (m)	[mpréhəsε lápsaʃ]

82. Kinds of business

accounting services	kontabilitet (m)	[kontabilitét]
advertising	reklamë (f)	[rɛklámə]
advertising agency	agjenci reklamash (f)	[aɟɛntsí rɛklámaʃ]
air-conditioners	kondicioner (m)	[konditsionér]
airline	kompani ajrore (f)	[kompaní ajrórɛ]
alcoholic beverages	pije alkoolike (pl)	[píjɛ alkoólikɛ]
antiques (antique dealers)	antikitete (pl)	[antikitétɛ]
art gallery (contemporary ~)	galeri e artit (f)	[galɛrí ɛ ártit]
audit services	shërbime auditimi (pl)	[ʃərbíme auditími]
banking industry	industri bankare (f)	[industrí bankárɛ]
beauty salon	sallon bukurie (m)	[saɫón bukuríɛ]
bookshop	librari (f)	[librarí]
brewery	birrari (f)	[birarí]
business centre	qendër biznesi (f)	[céndər biznési]
business school	shkollë biznesi (f)	[ʃkóɫə biznési]
casino	kazino (f)	[kazíno]
chemist, pharmacy	farmaci (f)	[farmatsí]
cinema	kinema (f)	[kinɛmá]
construction	ndërtim (m)	[ndərtím]
consulting	konsulencë (f)	[konsuléntsə]
dental clinic	klinikë dentare (f)	[kliníkə dɛntárɛ]
design	dizajn (m)	[dizájn]
dry cleaners	pastrim kimik (m)	[pastrím kimík]
employment agency	agjenci punësimi (f)	[aɟɛntsí punəsími]
financial services	shërbime financiare (pl)	[ʃərbíme finantsiárɛ]
food products	mallra ushqimore (f)	[máɫra uʃcimórɛ]
furniture (e.g. house ~)	orendi (f)	[orɛndí]
clothing, garment	rroba (f)	[róba]
hotel	hotel (m)	[hotél]
ice-cream	akullore (f)	[akuɫórɛ]
industry (manufacturing)	industri (f)	[industrí]
insurance	sigurim (m)	[sigurím]
Internet	internet (m)	[intɛrnét]
investments (finance)	investim (m)	[invɛstím]
jeweller	argjendar (m)	[arɟɛndár]
jewellery	bizhuteri (f)	[biʒutɛrí]
laundry (shop)	lavanteri (f)	[lavantɛrí]
legal adviser	këshilltar ligjor (m)	[kəʃiɫtár liɟór]
light industry	industri e lehtë (f)	[industrí ɛ léhtə]
magazine	revistë (f)	[rɛvístə]
mail order selling	shitje me katalog (f)	[ʃítjɛ mɛ katalóg]
medicine	mjekësi (f)	[mjɛkəsí]
museum	muze (m)	[muzé]
news agency	agjenci lajmesh (f)	[aɟɛntsí lájmɛʃ]
newspaper	gazetë (f)	[gazétə]

nightclub	**klub nate** (m)	[klúb nátɛ]
oil (petroleum)	**naftë** (f)	[náftə]
courier services	**shërbime postare** (f)	[ʃərbímɛ postárɛ]
pharmaceutics	**industria farmaceutike** (f)	[industría farmatsɛutíkɛ]
printing (industry)	**shtyp** (m)	[ʃtyp]
pub	**lokal** (m)	[lokál]
publishing house	**shtëpi botuese** (f)	[ʃtəpí botúɛsɛ]
radio (~ station)	**radio** (f)	[rádio]
real estate	**patundshmëri** (f)	[patundʃmərí]
restaurant	**restorant** (m)	[rɛstoránt]
security company	**kompani sigurimi** (f)	[kompaní sigurími]
shop	**dyqan** (m)	[dycán]
sport	**sport** (m)	[sport]
stock exchange	**bursë** (f)	[búrsə]
supermarket	**supermarket** (m)	[supɛrmarkét]
swimming pool (public ~)	**pishinë** (f)	[piʃínə]
tailor shop	**rrobaqepësi** (f)	[robacɛpəsí]
television	**televizor** (m)	[tɛlɛvizór]
theatre	**teatër** (m)	[tɛátər]
trade (commerce)	**tregti** (f)	[trɛgtí]
transport companies	**transport** (m)	[transpórt]
travel	**udhëtim** (m)	[uðətím]
undertakers	**agjenci funeralesh** (f)	[aɟɛntsí funɛrálɛʃ]
veterinary surgeon	**veteriner** (m)	[vɛtɛrinér]
warehouse	**magazinë** (f)	[magazínə]
waste collection	**mbledhja e mbeturinave** (f)	[mbléðja ɛ mbɛturínavɛ]

Job. Business. Part 2

83. Show. Exhibition

exhibition, show	ekspozitë (f)	[ɛkspozítə]
trade show	panair (m)	[panaír]
participation	pjesëmarrje (f)	[pjɛsəmárjɛ]
to participate (vi)	marr pjesë	[mar pjésə]
participant (exhibitor)	pjesëmarrës (m)	[pjɛsəmárəs]
director	drejtor (m)	[drɛjtór]
organizers' office	zyra drejtuese (f)	[zýra drɛjtúɛsɛ]
organizer	organizator (m)	[organizatór]
to organize (vt)	organizoj	[organizój]
participation form	kërkesë për pjesëmarrje (f)	[kərkésə pər pjɛsəmárjɛ]
to fill in (vt)	plotësoj	[plotəsój]
details	hollësi (pl)	[hoɫəsí]
information	informacion (m)	[informatsión]
price (cost, rate)	çmim (m)	[tʃmím]
including	përfshirë	[pərfʃírə]
to include (vt)	përfshij	[pərfʃíj]
to pay (vi, vt)	paguaj	[pagúaj]
registration fee	taksa e regjistrimit (f)	[táksa ɛ rɛɟistrímit]
entrance	hyrje (f)	[hýrjɛ]
pavilion, hall	pavijon (m)	[pavijón]
to register (vt)	regjistroj	[rɛɟistrój]
badge (identity tag)	kartë identifikimi (f)	[kártə idɛntifikími]
stand	kioskë (f)	[kióskə]
to reserve, to book	rezervoj	[rɛzɛrvój]
display case	vitrinë (f)	[vitrínə]
spotlight	dritë (f)	[drítə]
design	dizajn (m)	[dizájn]
to place (put, set)	vendos	[vɛndós]
to be placed	vendosur	[vɛndósur]
distributor	distributor (m)	[distributór]
supplier	furnitor (m)	[furnitór]
to supply (vt)	furnizoj	[furnizój]
country	shtet (m)	[ʃtɛt]
foreign (adj)	huaj	[húaj]
product	produkt (m)	[prodúkt]
association	shoqatë (f)	[ʃocátə]
conference hall	sallë konference (f)	[sáɫə konfɛréntsɛ]

| congress | kongres (m) | [koŋrés] |
| contest (competition) | konkurs (m) | [konkúrs] |

visitor (attendee)	vizitor (m)	[vizitór]
to visit (attend)	vizitoj	[vizitój]
customer	klient (m)	[kliént]

84. Science. Research. Scientists

science	shkencë (f)	[ʃkéntsə]
scientific (adj)	shkencore	[ʃkɛntsórɛ]
scientist	shkencëtar (m)	[ʃkɛntsətár]
theory	teori (f)	[tɛorí]

axiom	aksiomë (f)	[aksiómə]
analysis	analizë (f)	[analízə]
to analyse (vt)	analizoj	[analizój]
argument (strong ~)	argument (m)	[argumént]
substance (matter)	substancë (f)	[substántsə]

hypothesis	hipotezë (f)	[hipotézə]
dilemma	dilemë (f)	[dilémə]
dissertation	disertacion (m)	[disɛrtatsión]
dogma	dogma (f)	[dógma]

doctrine	doktrinë (f)	[doktrínə]
research	kërkim (m)	[kərkím]
to research (vt)	kërkoj	[kərkój]
tests (laboratory ~)	analizë (f)	[analízə]
laboratory	laborator (m)	[laboratór]

method	metodë (f)	[mɛtódə]
molecule	molekulë (f)	[molɛkúlə]
monitoring	monitorim (m)	[monitorím]
discovery (act, event)	zbulim (m)	[zbulím]

postulate	postulat (m)	[postulát]
principle	parim (m)	[parím]
forecast	parashikim (m)	[paraʃikím]
to forecast (vt)	parashikoj	[paraʃikój]

synthesis	sintezë (f)	[sintézə]
trend (tendency)	trend (m)	[trɛnd]
theorem	teoremë (f)	[tɛorémə]

teachings	mësim (m)	[məsím]
fact	fakt (m)	[fakt]
expedition	ekspeditë (f)	[ɛkspɛdítə]
experiment	eksperiment (m)	[ɛkspɛrimént]

academician	akademik (m)	[akadɛmík]
bachelor (e.g. ~ of Arts)	baçelor (m)	[bátʃelor]
doctor (PhD)	doktor shkencash (m)	[doktór ʃkéntsaʃ]
Associate Professor	Profesor i Asociuar (m)	[profɛsór i asotsiúar]

Master (e.g. ~ of Arts)	**Master** (m)	[mastér]
professor	**profesor** (m)	[profɛsór]

Professions and occupations

job	**punë** (f)	[púnə]
staff (work force)	**staf** (m)	[staf]
personnel	**personel** (m)	[pɛrsonél]
career	**karrierë** (f)	[kariérə]
prospects (chances)	**mundësi** (f)	[mundəsí]
skills (mastery)	**aftësi** (f)	[aftəsí]
selection (screening)	**përzgjedhje** (f)	[pərzɟéðjɛ]
employment agency	**agjenci punësimi** (f)	[aɟɛntsí punəsími]
curriculum vitae, CV	**resume** (f)	[rɛsumé]
job interview	**intervistë punësimi** (f)	[intɛrvístə punəsími]
vacancy	**vend i lirë pune** (m)	[vɛnd i lírə púnɛ]
salary, pay	**rrogë** (f)	[rógə]
fixed salary	**rrogë fikse** (f)	[rógə fíksɛ]
pay, compensation	**pagesë** (f)	[pagésə]
position (job)	**post** (m)	[post]
duty (of an employee)	**detyrë** (f)	[dɛtýrə]
range of duties	**lista e detyrave** (f)	[lísta ɛ dɛtýravɛ]
busy (I'm ~)	**i zënë**	[i zə́nə]
to fire (dismiss)	**pushoj nga puna**	[puʃój ŋa púna]
dismissal	**pushim nga puna** (m)	[puʃím ŋa púna]
unemployment	**papunësi** (m)	[papunəsí]
unemployed (n)	**i papunë** (m)	[i papúnə]
retirement	**pension** (m)	[pɛnsión]
to retire (from job)	**dal në pension**	[dál nə pɛnsión]

director	**drejtor** (m)	[drɛjtór]
manager (director)	**drejtor** (m)	[drɛjtór]
boss	**bos** (m)	[bos]
superior	**epror** (m)	[ɛprór]
superiors	**eprorët** (pl)	[ɛprórət]
president	**president** (m)	[prɛsidént]
chairman	**kryetar** (m)	[kryɛtár]
deputy (substitute)	**zëvendës** (m)	[zəvéndəs]
assistant	**ndihmës** (m)	[ndíhməs]

| secretary | sekretar (m) | [sɛkrɛtár] |
| personal assistant | ndihmës personal (m) | [ndíhməs pɛrsonál] |

businessman	biznesmen (m)	[biznɛsmén]
entrepreneur	sipërmarrës (m)	[sipərmárəs]
founder	themelues (m)	[θɛmɛlúɛs]
to found (vt)	themeloj	[θɛmɛlój]

founding member	bashkëthemelues (m)	[baʃkəθɛmɛlúɛs]
partner	partner (m)	[partnér]
shareholder	aksioner (m)	[aksionér]

millionaire	milioner (m)	[milionér]
billionaire	bilioner (m)	[bilionér]
owner, proprietor	pronar (m)	[pronár]
landowner	pronar tokash (m)	[pronár tókaʃ]

client	klient (m)	[kliént]
regular client	klient i rregullt (m)	[kliént i réguɬt]
buyer (customer)	blerës (m)	[blérəs]
visitor	vizitor (m)	[vizitór]

professional (n)	profesionist (m)	[profɛsioníst]
expert	ekspert (m)	[ɛkspért]
specialist	specialist (m)	[spɛtsialíst]

| banker | bankier (m) | [bankiér] |
| broker | komisioner (m) | [komisionér] |

cashier	arkëtar (m)	[arkətár]
accountant	kontabilist (m)	[kontabilíst]
security guard	roje sigurimi (m)	[rójɛ sigurími]

investor	investitor (m)	[invɛstitór]
debtor	debitor (m)	[dɛbitór]
creditor	kreditor (m)	[krɛditór]
borrower	huamarrës (m)	[huamárəs]

| importer | importues (m) | [importúɛs] |
| exporter | eksportues (m) | [ɛksportúɛs] |

manufacturer	prodhues (m)	[proðúɛs]
distributor	distributor (m)	[distributór]
middleman	ndërmjetës (m)	[ndərmjétəs]

consultant	këshilltar (m)	[kəʃiɬtár]
sales representative	përfaqësues i shitjeve (m)	[pərfacəsúɛs i ʃitjévɛ]
agent	agjent (m)	[aɟént]
insurance agent	agjent sigurimesh (m)	[aɟént sigurímɛʃ]

87. Service professions

| cook | kuzhinier (m) | [kuʒiniér] |
| chef (kitchen chef) | shef kuzhine (m) | [ʃɛf kuʒínɛ] |

baker	**furrtar** (m)	[furtár]
barman	**banakier** (m)	[banakiér]
waiter	**kamerier** (m)	[kamεriér]
waitress	**kameriere** (f)	[kamεriérε]

lawyer, barrister	**avokat** (m)	[avokát]
lawyer (legal expert)	**jurist** (m)	[juríst]
notary public	**noter** (m)	[notér]

electrician	**elektricist** (m)	[εlεktritsíst]
plumber	**hidraulik** (m)	[hidraulík]
carpenter	**marangoz** (m)	[maraŋóz]

masseur	**masazhist** (m)	[masaʒíst]
masseuse	**masazhiste** (f)	[masaʒístε]
doctor	**mjek** (m)	[mjék]

taxi driver	**shofer taksie** (m)	[ʃofér taksíε]
driver	**shofer** (m)	[ʃofér]
delivery man	**postier** (m)	[postiér]

chambermaid	**pastruese** (f)	[pastrúεsε]
security guard	**roje sigurimi** (m)	[rójε sigurími]
flight attendant (fem.)	**stjuardesë** (f)	[stjuardésə]

schoolteacher	**mësues** (m)	[məsúεs]
librarian	**punonjës biblioteke** (m)	[punóɲəs bibliotékε]
translator	**përkthyes** (m)	[pərkθýεs]
interpreter	**përkthyes** (m)	[pərkθýεs]
guide	**udhërrëfyes** (m)	[uðərəfýεs]

hairdresser	**parukiere** (f)	[parukiérε]
postman	**postier** (m)	[postiér]
salesman (store staff)	**shitës** (m)	[ʃítəs]

gardener	**kopshtar** (m)	[kopʃtár]
domestic servant	**shërbëtor** (m)	[ʃərbətór]
maid (female servant)	**shërbëtore** (f)	[ʃərbətórε]
cleaner (cleaning lady)	**pastruese** (f)	[pastrúεsε]

88. Military professions and ranks

private	**ushtar** (m)	[uʃtár]
sergeant	**rreshter** (m)	[rεʃtér]
lieutenant	**toger** (m)	[togér]
captain	**kapiten** (m)	[kapitén]

major	**major** (m)	[majór]
colonel	**kolonel** (m)	[kolonél]
general	**gjeneral** (m)	[ɟεnεrál]
marshal	**marshall** (m)	[marʃáɫ]
admiral	**admiral** (m)	[admirál]
military (n)	**ushtri** (f)	[uʃtrí]
soldier	**ushtar** (m)	[uʃtár]

| officer | oficer (m) | [ofitsér] |
| commander | komandant (m) | [komandánt] |

border guard	roje kufiri (m)	[rójɛ kufíri]
radio operator	radist (m)	[radíst]
scout (searcher)	eksplorues (m)	[ɛksplorúɛs]
pioneer (sapper)	xhenier (m)	[dʒɛniér]
marksman	shënjues (m)	[ʃəɲúɛs]
navigator	navigues (m)	[navigúɛs]

89. Officials. Priests

| king | mbret (m) | [mbrét] |
| queen | mbretëreshë (f) | [mbrɛtəréʃə] |

| prince | princ (m) | [prints] |
| princess | princeshë (f) | [printséʃə] |

| czar | car (m) | [tsár] |
| czarina | carina (f) | [tsarína] |

president	president (m)	[prɛsidént]
Secretary (minister)	ministër (m)	[minístər]
prime minister	kryeministër (m)	[kryɛminístər]
senator	senator (m)	[sɛnatór]

diplomat	diplomat (m)	[diplomát]
consul	konsull (m)	[kónsuɫ]
ambassador	ambasador (m)	[ambasadór]
counselor (diplomatic officer)	këshilltar diplomatik (m)	[kəʃiɫtár diplomatík]

official, functionary (civil servant)	zyrtar (m)	[zyrtár]
prefect	prefekt (m)	[prɛfékt]
mayor	kryetar komune (m)	[kryɛtár komúnɛ]

| judge | gjykatës (m) | [ɟykátəs] |
| prosecutor | prokuror (m) | [prokurór] |

missionary	misionar (m)	[misionár]
monk	murg (m)	[murg]
abbot	abat (m)	[abát]
rabbi	rabin (m)	[rabín]

vizier	vezir (m)	[vɛzír]
shah	shah (m)	[ʃah]
sheikh	sheik (m)	[ʃéik]

90. Agricultural professions

| beekeeper | bletar (m) | [blɛtár] |
| shepherd | bari (m) | [barí] |

agronomist	**agronom** (m)	[agronóm]
cattle breeder	**rritës bagëtish** (m)	[rítəs bagətíʃ]
veterinary surgeon	**veteriner** (m)	[vɛtɛrinér]
farmer	**fermer** (m)	[fɛrmér]
winemaker	**prodhues verërash** (m)	[proðúɛs véʁəraʃ]
zoologist	**zoolog** (m)	[zoológ]
cowboy	**lopar** (m)	[lopár]

91. Art professions

actor	**aktor** (m)	[aktór]
actress	**aktore** (f)	[aktórɛ]
singer (masc.)	**këngëtar** (m)	[kəŋətár]
singer (fem.)	**këngëtare** (f)	[kəŋətárɛ]
dancer (masc.)	**valltar** (m)	[vaɬtár]
dancer (fem.)	**valltare** (f)	[vaɬtárɛ]
performer (masc.)	**artist** (m)	[artíst]
performer (fem.)	**artiste** (f)	[artístɛ]
musician	**muzikant** (m)	[muzikánt]
pianist	**pianist** (m)	[pianíst]
guitar player	**kitarist** (m)	[kitaríst]
conductor (orchestra ~)	**dirigjent** (m)	[diriɟént]
composer	**kompozitor** (m)	[kompozitór]
impresario	**organizator** (m)	[organizatór]
film director	**regjisor** (m)	[rɛɟisór]
producer	**producent** (m)	[produtsént]
scriptwriter	**skenarist** (m)	[skɛnaríst]
critic	**kritik** (m)	[kritík]
writer	**shkrimtar** (m)	[ʃkrimtár]
poet	**poet** (m)	[poét]
sculptor	**skulptor** (m)	[skulptór]
artist (painter)	**piktor** (m)	[piktór]
juggler	**zhongler** (m)	[ʒoŋlér]
clown	**kloun** (m)	[kloún]
acrobat	**akrobat** (m)	[akrobát]
magician	**magjistar** (m)	[maɟistár]

92. Various professions

doctor	**mjek** (m)	[mjék]
nurse	**infermiere** (f)	[infɛrmiérɛ]
psychiatrist	**psikiatër** (m)	[psikiátər]
dentist	**dentist** (m)	[dɛntíst]

surgeon	kirurg (m)	[kirúrg]
astronaut	astronaut (m)	[astronaút]
astronomer	astronom (m)	[astronóm]
pilot	pilot (m)	[pilót]

driver (of a taxi, etc.)	shofer (m)	[ʃofér]
train driver	makinist (m)	[makiníst]
mechanic	mekanik (m)	[mɛkaník]

miner	minator (m)	[minatór]
worker	punëtor (m)	[punətór]
locksmith	bravandreqës (m)	[bravandrécəs]
joiner (carpenter)	marangoz (m)	[maraŋóz]
turner (lathe operator)	tornitor (m)	[tornitór]
building worker	punëtor ndërtimi (m)	[punətór ndərtími]
welder	saldator (m)	[saldatór]

professor (title)	profesor (m)	[profɛsór]
architect	arkitekt (m)	[arkitékt]
historian	historian (m)	[historián]
scientist	shkencëtar (m)	[ʃkɛntsətár]
physicist	fizikant (m)	[fizikánt]
chemist (scientist)	kimist (m)	[kimíst]

archaeologist	arkeolog (m)	[arkɛológ]
geologist	gjeolog (m)	[ɟɛológ]
researcher (scientist)	studiues (m)	[studiúɛs]

| babysitter | dado (f) | [dádo] |
| teacher, educator | mësues (m) | [məsúɛs] |

editor	redaktor (m)	[rɛdaktór]
editor-in-chief	kryeredaktor (m)	[kryɛrɛdaktór]
correspondent	korrespondent (m)	[korɛspondént]
typist (fem.)	daktilografiste (f)	[daktilografístɛ]

designer	projektues (m)	[projɛktúɛs]
computer expert	ekspert kompjuterësh (m)	[ɛkspért kompjutérəʃ]
programmer	programues (m)	[programúɛs]
engineer (designer)	inxhinier (m)	[indʒiniér]

sailor	marinar (m)	[marinár]
seaman	marinar (m)	[marinár]
rescuer	shpëtimtar (m)	[ʃpətimtár]

firefighter	zjarrfikës (m)	[zjarrfíkəs]
police officer	polic (m)	[políts]
watchman	roje (f)	[rójɛ]
detective	detektiv (m)	[dɛtɛktív]

customs officer	doganier (m)	[doganiér]
bodyguard	truprojë (f)	[truprójə]
prison officer	gardian burgu (m)	[gardián búrgu]
inspector	inspektor (m)	[inspɛktór]
sportsman	sportist (m)	[sportíst]
trainer, coach	trajner (m)	[trajnér]

butcher	kasap (m)	[kasáp]
cobbler (shoe repairer)	këpucëtar (m)	[kəputsətár]
merchant	tregtar (m)	[trɛgtár]
loader (person)	ngarkues (m)	[ŋarkúɛs]

| fashion designer | stilist (m) | [stilíst] |
| model (fem.) | modele (f) | [modélɛ] |

93. Occupations. Social status

| schoolboy | nxënës (m) | [ndzénəs] |
| student (college ~) | student (m) | [studént] |

philosopher	filozof (m)	[filozóf]
economist	ekonomist (m)	[ɛkonomíst]
inventor	shpikës (m)	[ʃpíkəs]

unemployed (n)	i papunë (m)	[i papúnə]
retiree, pensioner	pensionist (m)	[pɛnsioníst]
spy, secret agent	spiun (m)	[spiún]

prisoner	i burgosur (m)	[i burgósur]
striker	grevist (m)	[grɛvíst]
bureaucrat	burokrat (m)	[burokrát]
traveller (globetrotter)	udhëtar (m)	[uðətár]

gay, homosexual (n)	homoseksual (m)	[homosɛksuál]
hacker	haker (m)	[hakér]
hippie	hipik (m)	[hipík]

bandit	bandit (m)	[bandít]
hit man, killer	vrasës (m)	[vrásəs]
drug addict	narkoman (m)	[narkomán]
drug dealer	trafikant droge (m)	[trafikánt drógɛ]
prostitute (fem.)	prostitutë (f)	[prostitútə]
pimp	tutor (m)	[tutór]

sorcerer	magjistar (m)	[maɟistár]
sorceress (evil ~)	shtrigë (f)	[ʃtrígə]
pirate	pirat (m)	[pirát]
slave	skllav (m)	[skłav]
samurai	samurai (m)	[samurái]
savage (primitive)	i egër (m)	[i égər]

Education

school	**shkollë** (f)	[ʃkółə]
headmaster	**drejtor shkolle** (m)	[drɛjtór ʃkółɛ]
student (m)	**nxënës** (m)	[ndzénəs]
student (f)	**nxënëse** (f)	[ndzénəsɛ]
schoolboy	**nxënës** (m)	[ndzénəs]
schoolgirl	**nxënëse** (f)	[ndzénəsɛ]
to teach (sb)	**jap mësim**	[jap məsím]
to learn (language, etc.)	**mësoj**	[məsój]
to learn by heart	**mësoj përmendësh**	[məsój pərméndəʃ]
to learn (~ to count, etc.)	**mësoj**	[məsój]
to be at school	**jam në shkollë**	[jam nə ʃkółə]
to go to school	**shkoj në shkollë**	[ʃkoj nə ʃkółə]
alphabet	**alfabet** (m)	[alfabét]
subject (at school)	**lëndë** (f)	[léndə]
classroom	**klasë** (f)	[klásə]
lesson	**mësim** (m)	[məsím]
playtime, break	**pushim** (m)	[puʃím]
school bell	**zile e shkollës** (f)	[zílɛ ɛ ʃkółəs]
school desk	**bankë e shkollës** (f)	[bánkə ɛ ʃkółəs]
blackboard	**tabelë e zezë** (f)	[tabélə ɛ zézə]
mark	**notë** (f)	[nótə]
good mark	**notë e mirë** (f)	[nótə ɛ mírə]
bad mark	**notë e keqe** (f)	[nótə ɛ kécɛ]
to give a mark	**vendos notë**	[vɛndós nótə]
mistake, error	**gabim** (m)	[gabím]
to make mistakes	**bëj gabime**	[bəj gabímɛ]
to correct (an error)	**korrigjoj**	[koriɟój]
crib	**kopje** (f)	[kópjɛ]
homework	**detyrë shtëpie** (f)	[dɛtýrə ʃtəpíɛ]
exercise (in education)	**ushtrim** (m)	[uʃtrím]
to be present	**jam prezent**	[jam prɛzént]
to be absent	**mungoj**	[muɲój]
to miss school	**mungoj në shkollë**	[muɲój nə ʃkółə]
to punish (vt)	**ndëshkoj**	[ndəʃkój]
punishment	**ndëshkim** (m)	[ndəʃkím]
conduct (behaviour)	**sjellje** (f)	[sjéɫjɛ]

school report	**dëftesë** (f)	[dəftésə]
pencil	**laps** (m)	[láps]
rubber	**gomë** (f)	[gómə]
chalk	**shkumës** (m)	[ʃkúməs]
pencil case	**portofol lapsash** (m)	[portofól lápsaʃ]
schoolbag	**çantë shkolle** (f)	[tʃántə ʃkółɛ]
pen	**stilolaps** (m)	[stiloláps]
exercise book	**fletore** (f)	[flɛtórɛ]
textbook	**tekst mësimor** (m)	[tɛkst məsimór]
compasses	**kompas** (m)	[kompás]
to make technical drawings	**vizatoj**	[vizatój]
technical drawing	**vizatim teknik** (m)	[vizatím tɛkník]
poem	**poezi** (f)	[poɛzí]
by heart (adv)	**përmendësh**	[pərméndəʃ]
to learn by heart	**mësoj përmendësh**	[məsój pərméndəʃ]
school holidays	**pushimet e shkollës** (m)	[puʃímɛt ɛ ʃkółəs]
to be on holiday	**jam me pushime**	[jam mɛ puʃímɛ]
to spend holidays	**kaloj pushimet**	[kalój puʃímɛt]
test (at school)	**test** (m)	[tɛst]
essay (composition)	**ese** (f)	[ɛsé]
dictation	**diktim** (m)	[diktím]
exam (examination)	**provim** (m)	[provím]
to do an exam	**kam provim**	[kam provím]
experiment (e.g., chemistry ~)	**eksperiment** (m)	[ɛkspɛrimént]

95. College. University

academy	**akademi** (f)	[akadɛmí]
university	**universitet** (m)	[univɛrsitét]
faculty (e.g., ~ of Medicine)	**fakultet** (m)	[fakultét]
student (masc.)	**student** (m)	[studént]
student (fem.)	**studente** (f)	[studéntɛ]
lecturer (teacher)	**pedagog** (m)	[pɛdagóg]
lecture hall, room	**auditor** (m)	[auditór]
graduate	**i diplomuar** (m)	[i diplomúar]
diploma	**diplomë** (f)	[diplómə]
dissertation	**disertacion** (m)	[disɛrtatsión]
study (report)	**studim** (m)	[studím]
laboratory	**laborator** (m)	[laboratór]
lecture	**leksion** (m)	[lɛksión]
coursemate	**shok kursi** (m)	[ʃok kúrsi]
scholarship, bursary	**bursë** (f)	[búrsə]
academic degree	**diplomë akademike** (f)	[diplómə akadɛmíkɛ]

96. Sciences. Disciplines

mathematics	matematikë (f)	[matɛmatíkə]
algebra	algjebër (f)	[aljébər]
geometry	gjeometri (f)	[jɛomɛtrí]
astronomy	astronomi (f)	[astronomí]
biology	biologji (f)	[bioloʝí]
geography	gjeografi (f)	[jɛografí]
geology	gjeologji (f)	[jɛoloʝí]
history	histori (f)	[historí]
medicine	mjekësi (f)	[mjɛkəsí]
pedagogy	pedagogji (f)	[pɛdagoʝí]
law	drejtësi (f)	[drɛjtəsí]
physics	fizikë (f)	[fizíkə]
chemistry	kimi (f)	[kimí]
philosophy	filozofi (f)	[filozofí]
psychology	psikologji (f)	[psikoloʝí]

97. Writing system. Orthography

grammar	gramatikë (f)	[gramatíkə]
vocabulary	fjalor (m)	[fjalór]
phonetics	fonetikë (f)	[fonɛtíkə]
noun	emër (m)	[émər]
adjective	mbiemër (m)	[mbiémər]
verb	folje (f)	[fóljɛ]
adverb	ndajfolje (f)	[ndajfóljɛ]
pronoun	përemër (m)	[pərémər]
interjection	pasthirrmë (f)	[pasθírmə]
preposition	parafjalë (f)	[parafjálə]
root	rrënjë (f)	[réɲə]
ending	fundore (f)	[fundórɛ]
prefix	parashtesë (f)	[paraʃtésə]
syllable	rrokje (f)	[rókjɛ]
suffix	prapashtesë (f)	[prapaʃtésə]
stress mark	theks (m)	[θɛks]
apostrophe	apostrof (m)	[apostróf]
full stop	pikë (f)	[píkə]
comma	presje (f)	[présjɛ]
semicolon	pikëpresje (f)	[pikəprésjɛ]
colon	dy pika (f)	[dy píka]
ellipsis	tre pika (f)	[trɛ píka]
question mark	pikëpyetje (f)	[pikəpýɛtjɛ]
exclamation mark	pikëçuditje (f)	[pikətʃudítjɛ]

inverted commas	thonjëza (f)	[θóɲəza]
in inverted commas	në thonjëza	[nə θóɲəza]
parenthesis	kllapa (f)	[kɫápa]
in parenthesis	brenda kllapave	[brénda kɫápavɛ]

hyphen	vizë ndarëse (f)	[vízə ndárəsɛ]
dash	vizë (f)	[vízə]
space (between words)	hapësirë (f)	[hapəsírə]

| letter | shkronjë (f) | [ʃkróɲə] |
| capital letter | shkronjë e madhe (f) | [ʃkróɲə ɛ máðɛ] |

| vowel (n) | zanore (f) | [zanórɛ] |
| consonant (n) | bashkëtingëllore (f) | [baʃkətiŋəɫórɛ] |

sentence	fjali (f)	[fjalí]
subject	kryefjalë (f)	[kryɛfjálə]
predicate	kallëzues (m)	[kaɫəzúɛs]

line	rresht (m)	[réʃt]
on a new line	rresht i ri	[réʃt i rí]
paragraph	paragraf (m)	[paragráf]

word	fjalë (f)	[fjálə]
group of words	grup fjalësh (m)	[grup fjáləʃ]
expression	shprehje (f)	[ʃpréhjɛ]
synonym	sinonim (m)	[sinoním]
antonym	antonim (m)	[antoním]

rule	rregull (m)	[réguɫ]
exception	përjashtim (m)	[pərjaʃtím]
correct (adj)	saktë	[sáktə]

conjugation	lakim (m)	[lakím]
declension	rasë	[rásə]
nominal case	rasë emërore (f)	[rásə ɛmərórɛ]
question	pyetje (f)	[pýɛtjɛ]
to underline (vt)	nënvijëzoj	[nənvijəzój]
dotted line	vijë me ndërprerje (f)	[víjə mɛ ndərprérjɛ]

98. Foreign languages

language	gjuhë (f)	[ɟúhə]
foreign (adj)	huaj	[húaj]
foreign language	gjuhë e huaj (f)	[ɟúhə ɛ húaj]
to study (vt)	studioj	[studiój]
to learn (language, etc.)	mësoj	[məsój]

to read (vi, vt)	lexoj	[lɛdzój]
to speak (vi, vt)	flas	[flas]
to understand (vt)	kuptoj	[kuptój]
to write (vt)	shkruaj	[ʃkrúaj]
fast (adv)	shpejt	[ʃpɛjt]
slowly (adv)	ngadalë	[ŋadálə]

fluently (adv)	**rrjedhshëm**	[rjéðʃəm]
rules	**rregullat** (pl)	[régułat]
grammar	**gramatikë** (f)	[gramatíkə]
vocabulary	**fjalor** (m)	[fjalór]
phonetics	**fonetikë** (f)	[fonɛtíkə]
textbook	**tekst mësimor** (m)	[tɛkst məsimór]
dictionary	**fjalor** (m)	[fjalór]
teach-yourself book	**libër i mësimit autodidakt** (m)	[líbər i məsímit autodidákt]
phrasebook	**libër frazeologjik** (m)	[líbər frazɛoloɟík]
cassette, tape	**kasetë** (f)	[kasétə]
videotape	**videokasetë** (f)	[vidɛokasétə]
CD, compact disc	**CD** (f)	[tsɛdé]
DVD	**DVD** (m)	[dividí]
alphabet	**alfabet** (m)	[alfabét]
to spell (vt)	**gërmëzoj**	[gərməzój]
pronunciation	**shqiptim** (m)	[ʃciptím]
accent	**aksent** (m)	[aksént]
with an accent	**me aksent**	[mɛ aksént]
without an accent	**pa aksent**	[pa aksént]
word	**fjalë** (f)	[fjálə]
meaning	**kuptim** (m)	[kuptím]
course (e.g. a French ~)	**kurs** (m)	[kurs]
to sign up	**regjistrohem**	[rɛɟistróhɛm]
teacher	**mësues** (m)	[məsúɛs]
translation (process)	**përkthim** (m)	[pərkθím]
translation (text, etc.)	**përkthim** (m)	[pərkθím]
translator	**përkthyes** (m)	[pərkθýɛs]
interpreter	**përkthyes** (m)	[pərkθýɛs]
polyglot	**poliglot** (m)	[poliglót]
memory	**kujtesë** (f)	[kujtésə]

Rest. Entertainment. Travel

99. Trip. Travel

tourism, travel	**turizëm** (m)	[turízəm]
tourist	**turist** (m)	[turíst]
trip, voyage	**udhëtim** (m)	[uðətím]
adventure	**aventurë** (f)	[avɛntúrə]
trip, journey	**udhëtim** (m)	[uðətím]
holiday	**pushim** (m)	[puʃím]
to be on holiday	**jam me pushime**	[jam mɛ puʃímɛ]
rest	**pushim** (m)	[puʃím]
train	**tren** (m)	[trɛn]
by train	**me tren**	[mɛ trén]
aeroplane	**avion** (m)	[avión]
by aeroplane	**me avion**	[mɛ avión]
by car	**me makinë**	[mɛ makínə]
by ship	**me anije**	[mɛ aníjɛ]
luggage	**bagazh** (m)	[bagáʒ]
suitcase	**valixhe** (f)	[valídʒɛ]
luggage trolley	**karrocë bagazhesh** (f)	[karótsə bagáʒɛʃ]
passport	**pasaportë** (f)	[pasapórtə]
visa	**vizë** (f)	[vízə]
ticket	**biletë** (f)	[bilétə]
air ticket	**biletë avioni** (f)	[bilétə avióni]
guidebook	**guidë turistike** (f)	[guídə turistíkɛ]
map (tourist ~)	**hartë** (f)	[hártə]
area (rural ~)	**zonë** (f)	[zónə]
place, site	**vend** (m)	[vɛnd]
exotica (n)	**ekzotikë** (f)	[ɛkzotíkə]
exotic (adj)	**ekzotik**	[ɛkzotík]
amazing (adj)	**mahnitëse**	[mahnítəsɛ]
group	**grup** (m)	[grup]
excursion, sightseeing tour	**ekskursion** (m)	[ɛkskursión]
guide (person)	**udhërrëfyes** (m)	[uðərəfýɛs]

100. Hotel

hotel	**hotel** (m)	[hotél]
motel	**motel** (m)	[motél]
three-star (~ hotel)	**me tre yje**	[mɛ trɛ ýjɛ]

five-star	me pesë yje	[mɛ pésə ýjɛ]
to stay (in a hotel, etc.)	qëndroj	[cəndrój]
room	dhomë (f)	[ðómə]
single room	dhomë teke (f)	[ðómə tékɛ]
double room	dhomë dyshe (f)	[ðómə dýʃɛ]
to book a room	rezervoj një dhomë	[rɛzɛrvój ɲə ðómə]
half board	gjysmë-pension (m)	[ɟýsmə-pɛnsión]
full board	pension i plotë (m)	[pɛnsión i plótə]
with bath	me banjo	[mɛ báɲo]
with shower	me dush	[mɛ dúʃ]
satellite television	televizor satelitor (m)	[tɛlɛvizór satɛlitór]
air-conditioner	kondicioner (m)	[konditsionér]
towel	peshqir (m)	[pɛʃcír]
key	çelës (m)	[tʃéləs]
administrator	administrator (m)	[administratór]
chambermaid	pastruese (f)	[pastrúɛsɛ]
porter	portier (m)	[portiér]
doorman	portier (m)	[portiér]
restaurant	restorant (m)	[rɛstoránt]
pub, bar	pab (m), pijetore (f)	[pab], [pijɛtórɛ]
breakfast	mëngjes (m)	[mənɟés]
dinner	darkë (f)	[dárkə]
buffet	bufe (f)	[bufé]
lobby	holl (m)	[hoɫ]
lift	ashensor (m)	[aʃɛnsór]
DO NOT DISTURB	MOS SHQETËSONI	[mos ʃcɛtəsóni]
NO SMOKING	NDALOHET DUHANI	[ndalóhɛt duháni]

TECHNICAL EQUIPMENT. TRANSPORT

Technical equipment

101. Computer

computer	**kompjuter** (m)	[kompjutér]
notebook, laptop	**laptop** (m)	[laptóp]
to turn on	**ndez**	[ndɛz]
to turn off	**fik**	[fik]
keyboard	**tastiera** (f)	[tastiéra]
key	**çelës** (m)	[tʃéləs]
mouse	**maus** (m)	[máus]
mouse mat	**shtroje e mausit** (f)	[ʃtrójɛ ɛ máusit]
button	**buton** (m)	[butón]
cursor	**kursor** (m)	[kursór]
monitor	**monitor** (m)	[monitór]
screen	**ekran** (m)	[ɛkrán]
hard disk	**hard disk** (m)	[hárd dísk]
hard disk capacity	**kapaciteti i hard diskut** (m)	[kapatsitéti i hárd dískut]
memory	**memorie** (f)	[mɛmóriɛ]
random access memory	**memorie operative** (f)	[mɛmóriɛ opɛratívɛ]
file	**skedë** (f)	[skédə]
folder	**dosje** (f)	[dósjɛ]
to open (vt)	**hap**	[hap]
to close (vt)	**mbyll**	[mbyɫ]
to save (vt)	**ruaj**	[rúaj]
to delete (vt)	**fshij**	[fʃíj]
to copy (vt)	**kopjoj**	[kopjój]
to sort (vt)	**sistemoj**	[sistɛmój]
to transfer (copy)	**transferoj**	[transfɛrój]
programme	**program** (m)	[prográm]
software	**softuer** (f)	[softuér]
programmer	**programues** (m)	[programúɛs]
to program (vt)	**programoj**	[programój]
hacker	**haker** (m)	[hakér]
password	**fjalëkalim** (m)	[fjaləkalím]
virus	**virus** (m)	[virús]
to find, to detect	**zbuloj**	[zbulój]
byte	**bajt** (m)	[bájt]

megabyte	megabajt (m)	[mɛgabájt]
data	të dhënat (pl)	[tə ðə́nat]
database	databazë (f)	[databázə]

cable (USB, etc.)	kabllo (f)	[kábɬo]
to disconnect (vt)	shkëpus	[ʃkəpús]
to connect (sth to sth)	lidh	[liδ]

102. Internet. E-mail

Internet	internet (m)	[intɛrnét]
browser	shfletues (m)	[ʃflɛtúɛs]
search engine	makineri kërkimi (f)	[makinɛrí kərkími]
provider	ofrues (m)	[ofrúɛs]

webmaster	uebmaster (m)	[uɛbmástɛr]
website	ueb-faqe (f)	[uéb-fácɛ]
web page	ueb-faqe (f)	[uéb-fácɛ]

| address (e-mail ~) | adresë (f) | [adrésə] |
| address book | libërth adresash (m) | [líbərθ adrésaʃ] |

postbox	kuti postare (f)	[kutí postárɛ]
post	postë (f)	[póstə]
full (adj)	i mbushur	[i mbúʃur]

message	mesazh (m)	[mɛsáʒ]
incoming messages	mesazhe të ardhura (pl)	[mɛsáʒɛ tə árðura]
outgoing messages	mesazhe të dërguara (pl)	[mɛsáʒɛ tə dərgúara]

sender	dërguesi (m)	[dərgúɛsi]
to send (vt)	dërgoj	[dərgój]
sending (of mail)	dërgesë (f)	[dərgésə]

| receiver | pranues (m) | [pranúɛs] |
| to receive (vt) | pranoj | [pranój] |

| correspondence | korrespondencë (f) | [korɛspondéntsə] |
| to correspond (vi) | komunikim | [komunikím] |

file	skedë (f)	[skédə]
to download (vt)	shkarkoj	[ʃkarkój]
to create (vt)	krijoj	[krijój]
to delete (vt)	fshij	[fʃíj]
deleted (adj)	e fshirë	[ɛ fʃírə]

connection (ADSL, etc.)	lidhje (f)	[líδjɛ]
speed	shpejtësi (f)	[ʃpɛjtəsí]
modem	modem (m)	[modém]
access	hyrje (f)	[hýrjɛ]
port (e.g. input ~)	port (m)	[port]

| connection (make a ~) | lidhje (f) | [líδjɛ] |
| to connect to … (vi) | lidhem me … | [líδɛm mɛ …] |

| to select (vt) | përzgjedh | [pərzɟéð] |
| to search (for ...) | kërkoj ... | [kərkój ...] |

103. Electricity

electricity	elektricitet (m)	[ɛlɛktritsitét]
electric, electrical (adj)	elektrik	[ɛlɛktrík]
electric power station	hidrocentral (m)	[hidrotsɛntrál]
energy	energji (f)	[ɛnɛɟí]
electric power	energji elektrike (f)	[ɛnɛɟí ɛlɛktríkɛ]

light bulb	poç (m)	[potʃ]
torch	llambë dore (f)	[łámbə dórɛ]
street light	llambë rruge (f)	[łámbə rúgɛ]

light	dritë (f)	[drítə]
to turn on	ndez	[ndɛz]
to turn off	fik	[fik]
to turn off the light	fik dritën	[fík drítən]

to burn out (vi)	digjet	[díɟɛt]
short circuit	qark i shkurtër (m)	[cark i ʃkúrtər]
broken wire	tel i prishur (m)	[tɛl i príʃur]
contact (electrical ~)	kontakt (m)	[kontákt]

light switch	çelës drite (m)	[tʃéləs drítɛ]
socket outlet	prizë (f)	[prízə]
plug	spinë (f)	[spínə]
extension lead	zgjatues (m)	[zɟatúɛs]

fuse	siguresë (f)	[sigurésə]
cable, wire	kabllo (f)	[kábło]
wiring	rrjet elektrik (m)	[rjét ɛlɛktrík]

ampere	amper (m)	[ampér]
amperage	amperazh (f)	[ampɛráʒ]
volt	volt (m)	[volt]
voltage	voltazh (m)	[voltáʒ]

| electrical device | aparat elektrik (m) | [aparát ɛlɛktrík] |
| indicator | indikator (m) | [indikatór] |

electrician	elektricist (m)	[ɛlɛktritsíst]
to solder (vt)	saldoj	[saldój]
soldering iron	pajisje saldimi (f)	[pajísjɛ saldími]
electric current	korrent elektrik (m)	[korént ɛlɛktrík]

104. Tools

tool, instrument	vegël (f)	[végəl]
tools	vegla (pl)	[végla]
equipment (factory ~)	pajisje (f)	[pajísjɛ]

hammer	çekiç (m)	[tʃɛkítʃ]
screwdriver	kaçavidë (f)	[katʃavídə]
axe	sëpatë (f)	[səpátə]

saw	sharrë (f)	[ʃárə]
to saw (vt)	sharroj	[ʃarój]
plane (tool)	zdrukthues (m)	[zdrukθúɛs]
to plane (vt)	zdrukthoj	[zdrukθój]
soldering iron	pajisje saldimi (f)	[pajísjɛ saldími]
to solder (vt)	saldoj	[saldój]

file (tool)	limë (f)	[límə]
carpenter pincers	darë (f)	[dárə]
combination pliers	pinca (f)	[píntsa]
chisel	daltë (f)	[dáltə]

drill bit	turjelë (f)	[turjélə]
electric drill	shpuese elektrike (f)	[ʃpúɛsɛ ɛlɛktríkɛ]
to drill (vi, vt)	shpoj	[ʃpoj]

knife	thikë (f)	[θíkə]
pocket knife	thikë xhepi (f)	[θíkə dʒépi]
blade	teh (m)	[tɛh]

sharp (blade, etc.)	i mprehtë	[i mpréhtə]
dull, blunt (adj)	i topitur	[i topítur]
to get blunt (dull)	bëhet e topitur	[bə́hɛt ɛ topítur]
to sharpen (vt)	mpreh	[mpréh]

bolt	vidë (f)	[vídə]
nut	dado (f)	[dádo]
thread (of a screw)	filetë e vidhës (f)	[filétə ɛ víðəs]
wood screw	vidhë druri (f)	[víðə drúri]

| nail | gozhdë (f) | [góʒdə] |
| nailhead | kokë gozhde (f) | [kókə góʒdɛ] |

ruler (for measuring)	vizore (f)	[vizórɛ]
tape measure	metër (m)	[métər]
spirit level	nivelizues (m)	[nivɛlizúɛs]
magnifying glass	lente zmadhuese (f)	[léntɛ zmaðúɛsɛ]

measuring instrument	mjet matës (m)	[mjét mátəs]
to measure (vt)	mas	[mas]
scale (temperature ~, etc.)	gradë (f)	[grádə]
readings	matjet (pl)	[mátjɛt]

| compressor | kompresor (m) | [komprɛsór] |
| microscope | mikroskop (m) | [mikroskóp] |

pump (e.g. water ~)	pompë (f)	[pómpə]
robot	robot (m)	[robót]
laser	laser (m)	[lasér]

| spanner | çelës (m) | [tʃéləs] |
| adhesive tape | shirit ngjitës (m) | [ʃirít ɲʝítəs] |

glue	ngjitës (m)	[ɲítəs]
sandpaper	letër smeril (f)	[létər smɛríl]
spring	sustë (f)	[sústə]
magnet	magnet (m)	[magnét]
gloves	dorëza (pl)	[dórəza]

rope	litar (m)	[litár]
cord	kordon (m)	[kordón]
wire (e.g. telephone ~)	tel (m)	[tɛl]
cable	kabllo (f)	[kábɫo]

sledgehammer	çekan i rëndë (m)	[tʃɛkán i rəndə]
prybar	levë (f)	[lévə]
ladder	shkallë (f)	[ʃkáɫə]
stepladder	shkallëz (f)	[ʃkáɫəz]

to screw (tighten)	vidhos	[viðós]
to unscrew (lid, filter, etc.)	zhvidhos	[ʒviðós]
to tighten (e.g. with a clamp)	shtrëngoj	[ʃtrəɲój]
to glue, to stick	ngjes	[ɲés]
to cut (vt)	pres	[prɛs]

malfunction (fault)	avari (f)	[avarí]
repair (mending)	riparim (m)	[riparím]
to repair, to fix (vt)	riparoj	[riparój]
to adjust (machine, etc.)	rregulloj	[rɛguɫój]

to check (to examine)	kontrolloj	[kontroɫój]
checking	kontroll (m)	[kontróɫ]
readings	matjet (pl)	[mátjɛt]

| reliable, solid (machine) | e sigurt | [ɛ sígurt] |
| complex (adj) | komplekse | [kompléksɛ] |

to rust (get rusted)	ndryshket	[ndrýʃkɛt]
rusty (adj)	e ndryshkur	[ɛ ndrýʃkur]
rust	ndryshk (m)	[ndrýʃk]

Transport

aeroplane	**avion** (m)	[avión]
air ticket	**biletë avioni** (f)	[bilétə avióni]
airline	**kompani ajrore** (f)	[kompaní ajrórɛ]
airport	**aeroport** (m)	[aɛropórt]
supersonic (adj)	**supersonik**	[supɛrsoník]
captain	**kapiten** (m)	[kapitén]
crew	**ekip** (m)	[ɛkíp]
pilot	**pilot** (m)	[pilót]
stewardess	**stjuardesë** (f)	[stjuardésə]
navigator	**navigues** (m)	[navigúɛs]
wings	**krahë** (pl)	[kráhə]
tail	**bisht** (m)	[biʃt]
cockpit	**kabinë** (f)	[kabínə]
engine	**motor** (m)	[motór]
undercarriage (landing gear)	**karrel** (m)	[karél]
turbine	**turbinë** (f)	[turbínə]
propeller	**helikë** (f)	[hɛlíkə]
black box	**kuti e zezë** (f)	[kutí ɛ zézə]
yoke (control column)	**timon** (m)	[timón]
fuel	**karburant** (m)	[karburánt]
safety card	**udhëzime sigurie** (pl)	[uðəzímɛ siguríɛ]
oxygen mask	**maskë oksigjeni** (f)	[máskə oksiɟéni]
uniform	**uniformë** (f)	[unifórmə]
lifejacket	**jelek shpëtimi** (m)	[jɛlék ʃpətími]
parachute	**parashutë** (f)	[paraʃútə]
takeoff	**ngritje** (f)	[ŋrítjɛ]
to take off (vi)	**fluturon**	[fluturón]
runway	**pista e fluturimit** (f)	[písta ɛ fluturímit]
visibility	**shikueshmëri** (f)	[ʃikuɛʃmərí]
flight (act of flying)	**fluturim** (m)	[fluturím]
altitude	**lartësi** (f)	[lartəsí]
air pocket	**xhep ajri** (m)	[dʒɛp ájri]
seat	**karrige** (f)	[karígɛ]
headphones	**kufje** (f)	[kúfjɛ]
folding tray (tray table)	**tabaka** (f)	[tabaká]
airplane window	**dritare avioni** (f)	[dritárɛ avióni]
aisle	**korridor** (m)	[koridór]

106. Train

train	tren (m)	[trɛn]
commuter train	tren elektrik (m)	[trɛn ɛlɛktrík]
express train	tren ekspres (m)	[trɛn ɛksprés]
diesel locomotive	lokomotivë me naftë (f)	[lokomótivə mɛ náftə]
steam locomotive	lokomotivë me avull (f)	[lokomótivə mɛ ávuɫ]
coach, carriage	vagon (m)	[vagón]
buffet car	vagon restorant (m)	[vagón rɛstoránt]
rails	shina (pl)	[ʃína]
railway	hekurudhë (f)	[hɛkurúðə]
sleeper (track support)	traversë (f)	[travérsə]
platform (railway ~)	platformë (f)	[platfórmə]
platform (~ 1, 2, etc.)	binar (m)	[binár]
semaphore	semafor (m)	[sɛmafór]
station	stacion (m)	[statsión]
train driver	makinist (m)	[makiníst]
porter (of luggage)	portier (m)	[portiér]
carriage attendant	konduktor (m)	[konduktór]
passenger	pasagjer (m)	[pasaɟér]
ticket inspector	konduktor (m)	[konduktór]
corridor (in train)	korridor (m)	[koridór]
emergency brake	frena urgjence (f)	[fréna urɟéntsɛ]
compartment	ndarje (f)	[ndárjɛ]
berth	kat (m)	[kat]
upper berth	kati i sipërm (m)	[káti i sípərm]
lower berth	kati i poshtëm (m)	[káti i póʃtəm]
bed linen, bedding	shtroje shtrati (pl)	[ʃtrójɛ ʃtráti]
ticket	biletë (f)	[bilétə]
timetable	orar (m)	[orár]
information display	tabelë e informatave (f)	[tabélə ɛ informátavɛ]
to leave, to depart	niset	[nísɛt]
departure (of a train)	nisje (f)	[nísjɛ]
to arrive (ab. train)	arrij	[aríj]
arrival	arritje (f)	[arítjɛ]
to arrive by train	arrij me tren	[aríj mɛ trɛn]
to get on the train	hip në tren	[hip nə trén]
to get off the train	zbres nga treni	[zbrɛs ŋa tréni]
train crash	aksident hekurudhor (m)	[aksidént hɛkuruðór]
to derail (vi)	del nga shinat	[dɛl ŋa ʃínat]
steam locomotive	lokomotivë me avull (f)	[lokomótivə mɛ ávuɫ]
stoker, fireman	mbikëqyrës i zjarrit (m)	[mbikəçýrəs i zjárit]
firebox	furrë (f)	[fúrə]
coal	qymyr (m)	[cymýr]

107. Ship

ship	anije (f)	[aníjɛ]
vessel	mjet lundrues (m)	[mjét lundrúɛs]
steamship	anije me avull (f)	[aníjɛ mɛ ávuɫ]
riverboat	anije lumi (f)	[aníjɛ lúmi]
cruise ship	krocierë (f)	[krotsiérə]
cruiser	anije luftarake (f)	[aníjɛ luftarákɛ]
yacht	jaht (m)	[jáht]
tugboat	anije rimorkiuese (f)	[aníjɛ rimorkiúɛsɛ]
barge	anije transportuese (f)	[aníjɛ transportúɛsɛ]
ferry	traget (m)	[tragét]
sailing ship	anije me vela (f)	[aníjɛ mɛ véla]
brigantine	brigantinë (f)	[brigantínə]
ice breaker	akullthyese (f)	[akuɫθýɛsɛ]
submarine	nëndetëse (f)	[nəndétəsɛ]
boat (flat-bottomed ~)	barkë (f)	[bárkə]
dinghy (lifeboat)	gomone (f)	[gomónɛ]
lifeboat	varkë shpëtimi (f)	[várkə ʃpətími]
motorboat	skaf (m)	[skaf]
captain	kapiten (m)	[kapitén]
seaman	marinar (m)	[marinár]
sailor	marinar (m)	[marinár]
crew	ekip (m)	[ɛkíp]
boatswain	kryemarinar (m)	[kryɛmarinár]
ship's boy	djali i anijes (m)	[djáli i aníjɛs]
cook	kuzhinier (m)	[kuʒiniér]
ship's doctor	doktori i anijes (m)	[doktóri i aníjɛs]
deck	kuverta (f)	[kuvérta]
mast	direk (m)	[dirék]
sail	vela (f)	[véla]
hold	bagazh (m)	[bagáʒ]
bow (prow)	harku sipëror (m)	[hárku sipərór]
stern	pjesa e pasme (f)	[pjésa ɛ pásmɛ]
oar	rrem (m)	[rɛm]
screw propeller	helikë (f)	[hɛlíkə]
cabin	kabinë (f)	[kabínə]
wardroom	zyrë e oficerëve (m)	[zýrə ɛ ofitsérəvɛ]
engine room	salla e motorit (m)	[sáɫa ɛ motórit]
bridge	urë komanduese (f)	[úrə komandúɛsɛ]
radio room	kabina radiotelegrafike (f)	[kabína radiotɛlɛgrafíkɛ]
wave (radio)	valë (f)	[válə]
logbook	libri i shënimeve (m)	[líbri i ʃənímɛvɛ]
spyglass	dylbi (f)	[dylbí]
bell	këmbanë (f)	[kəmbánə]

flag	flamur (m)	[flamúr]
hawser (mooring ~)	pallamar (m)	[paɫamár]
knot (bowline, etc.)	nyjë (f)	[nýjə]

| deckrails | parmakë (pl) | [parmákə] |
| gangway | shkallë (f) | [ʃkáɫə] |

anchor	spirancë (f)	[spirántsə]
to weigh anchor	ngre spirancën	[ŋré spirántsən]
to drop anchor	hedh spirancën	[hɛð spirántsən]
anchor chain	zinxhir i spirancës (m)	[zindʒír i spirántsəs]

port (harbour)	port (m)	[port]
quay, wharf	skelë (f)	[skélə]
to berth (moor)	ankoroj	[ankorój]
to cast off	niset	[nísɛt]

trip, voyage	udhëtim (m)	[uðətím]
cruise (sea trip)	udhëtim me krocierë (f)	[uðətím mɛ krotsiérə]
course (route)	kursi i udhëtimit (m)	[kúrsi i uðətímit]
route (itinerary)	itinerar (m)	[itinɛrár]

fairway (safe water channel)	ujëra të lundrueshme (f)	[újəra tə lundrúɛʃmɛ]
shallows	cekëtinë (f)	[tsɛkətínə]
to run aground	bllokohet në rërë	[bɫokóhɛt nə rərə]

storm	stuhi (f)	[stuhí]
signal	sinjal (m)	[siɲál]
to sink (vi)	fundoset	[fundósɛt]
Man overboard!	Njeri në det!	[ɲɛrí nə dɛt!]
SOS (distress signal)	SOS (m)	[sos]
ring buoy	bovë shpëtuese (f)	[bóvə ʃpətúɛsɛ]

108. Airport

airport	aeroport (m)	[aɛropórt]
aeroplane	avion (m)	[avión]
airline	kompani ajrore (f)	[kompaní ajrórɛ]
air traffic controller	kontroll i trafikut ajror (m)	[kontróɫ i trafíkut ajrór]

departure	nisje (f)	[nísjɛ]
arrival	arritje (f)	[arítjɛ]
to arrive (by plane)	arrij me avion	[aríj mɛ avión]

| departure time | nisja (f) | [nísja] |
| arrival time | arritja (f) | [arítja] |

| to be delayed | vonesë | [vonésə] |
| flight delay | vonesë avioni (f) | [vonésə avióni] |

information board	ekrani i informacioneve (m)	[ɛkráni i informatsiónɛvɛ]
information	informacion (m)	[informatsión]
to announce (vt)	njoftoj	[ɲoftój]
flight (e.g. next ~)	fluturim (m)	[fluturím]

| customs | dogane (f) | [dogánə] |
| customs officer | doganier (m) | [doganiér] |

customs declaration	deklarim doganor (m)	[dɛklarím doganór]
to fill in (vt)	plotësoj	[plotəsój]
to fill in the declaration	plotësoj deklaratën	[plotəsój dɛklarátən]
passport control	kontroll pasaportash (m)	[kontrół pasapórtaʃ]

luggage	bagazh (m)	[bagáʒ]
hand luggage	bagazh dore (m)	[bagáʒ dórɛ]
luggage trolley	karrocë bagazhesh (f)	[karótsə bagáʒɛʃ]

landing	aterrim (m)	[atɛrím]
landing strip	pistë aterrimi (f)	[pístə atɛrími]
to land (vi)	aterroj	[atɛrój]
airstair (passenger stair)	shkallë avioni (f)	[ʃkáłə avióni]

check-in	regjistrim (m)	[rɛɟistrím]
check-in counter	sportel regjistrimi (m)	[sportél rɛɟistrími]
to check-in (vi)	regjistrohem	[rɛɟistróhɛm]
boarding card	biletë e hyrjes (f)	[bilétə ɛ hýrjɛs]
departure gate	porta e nisjes (f)	[pórta ɛ nísjɛs]

transit	transit (m)	[transít]
to wait (vt)	pres	[prɛs]
departure lounge	salla e nisjes (f)	[sáła ɛ nísjɛs]
to see off	përcjell	[pərtsjéł]
to say goodbye	përshëndetem	[pərʃəndétɛm]

Life events

celebration, holiday	festë (f)	[féstə]
national day	festë kombëtare (f)	[féstə kombətárɛ]
public holiday	festë publike (f)	[féstə publíkɛ]
to commemorate (vt)	festoj	[fɛstój]
event (happening)	ceremoni (f)	[tsɛrɛmoní]
event (organized activity)	eveniment (m)	[ɛvɛnimént]
banquet (party)	banket (m)	[bankét]
reception (formal party)	pritje (f)	[prítjɛ]
feast	aheng (m)	[ahén]
anniversary	përvjetor (m)	[pərvjɛtór]
jubilee	jubile (m)	[jubilé]
to celebrate (vt)	festoj	[fɛstój]
New Year	Viti i Ri (m)	[víti i rí]
Happy New Year!	Gëzuar Vitin e Ri!	[gəzúar vítin ɛ rí!]
Father Christmas	Santa Klaus (m)	[sánta kláus]
Christmas	Krishtlindje (f)	[kriʃtlíndjɛ]
Merry Christmas!	Gëzuar Krishtlindjen!	[gəzúar kriʃtlíndjɛn!]
Christmas tree	péma e Krishtlindjes (f)	[péma ɛ kriʃtlíndjɛs]
fireworks (fireworks show)	fishekzjarrë (m)	[fiʃɛkzjárə]
wedding	dasmë (f)	[dásmə]
groom	dhëndër (m)	[ðéndər]
bride	nuse (f)	[núsɛ]
to invite (vt)	ftoj	[ftoj]
invitation card	ftesë (f)	[ftésə]
guest	mysafir (m)	[mysafír]
to visit (~ your parents, etc.)	vizitoj	[vizitój]
to meet the guests	takoj të ftuarit	[takój tə ftúarit]
gift, present	dhuratë (f)	[ðurátə]
to give (sth as present)	dhuroj	[ðurój]
to receive gifts	marr dhurata	[mar ðuráta]
bouquet (of flowers)	buqetë (f)	[bucétə]
congratulations	urime (f)	[urímɛ]
to congratulate (vt)	përgëzoj	[pərgəzój]
greetings card	kartolinë (f)	[kartolínə]
to send a postcard	dërgoj kartolinë	[dərgój kartolínə]
to get a postcard	marr kartolinë	[mar kartolínə]

toast	dolli (f)	[doɫí]
to offer (a drink, etc.)	qeras	[cɛrás]
champagne	shampanjë (f)	[ʃampáɲə]

to enjoy oneself	kënaqem	[kənácɛm]
merriment (gaiety)	gëzim (m)	[gəzím]
joy (emotion)	gëzim (m)	[gəzím]

| dance | vallëzim (m) | [vaɫəzím] |
| to dance (vi, vt) | vallëzoj | [vaɫəzój] |

| waltz | vals (m) | [vals] |
| tango | tango (f) | [táŋo] |

110. Funerals. Burial

cemetery	varreza (f)	[varéza]
grave, tomb	varr (m)	[var]
cross	kryq (m)	[kryc]
gravestone	gur varri (m)	[gur vári]
fence	gardh (m)	[garð]
chapel	kishëz (m)	[kíʃəz]

death	vdekje (f)	[vdékjɛ]
to die (vi)	vdes	[vdɛs]
the deceased	i vdekuri (m)	[i vdékuri]
mourning	zi (f)	[zi]

to bury (vt)	varros	[varós]
undertakers	agjenci funeralesh (f)	[aɟentsí funɛráleʃ]
funeral	funeral (m)	[funɛrál]

wreath	kurorë (f)	[kurórə]
coffin	arkivol (m)	[arkivól]
hearse	makinë funebre (f)	[makínə funébrɛ]
shroud	qefin (m)	[cɛfín]

funeral procession	kortezh (m)	[kortéʒ]
funerary urn	urnë (f)	[úrnə]
crematorium	kremator (m)	[krɛmatór]

obituary	përkujtim (m)	[pərkujtím]
to cry (weep)	qaj	[caj]
to sob (vi)	qaj me dënesë	[caj mɛ dənésə]

111. War. Soldiers

platoon	togë (f)	[tógə]
company	kompani (f)	[kompaní]
regiment	regjiment (m)	[rɛɟimént]
army	ushtri (f)	[uʃtrí]
division	divizion (m)	[divizión]

| section, squad | skuadër (f) | [skuádər] |
| host (army) | armatë (f) | [armátə] |

| soldier | ushtar (m) | [uʃtár] |
| officer | oficer (m) | [ofitsér] |

private	ushtar (m)	[uʃtár]
sergeant	rreshter (m)	[rɛʃtér]
lieutenant	toger (m)	[togér]
captain	kapiten (m)	[kapitén]
major	major (m)	[majór]
colonel	kolonel (m)	[kolonél]
general	gjeneral (m)	[ɟɛnɛrál]

sailor	marinar (m)	[marinár]
captain	kapiten (m)	[kapitén]
boatswain	kryemarinar (m)	[kryɛmarinár]
artilleryman	artiljer (m)	[artiljér]
paratrooper	parashutist (m)	[paraʃutíst]
pilot	pilot (m)	[pilót]
navigator	navigues (m)	[navigúɛs]
mechanic	mekanik (m)	[mɛkaník]

pioneer (sapper)	xhenier (m)	[dʒɛniér]
parachutist	parashutist (m)	[paraʃutíst]
reconnaissance scout	agjent zbulimi (m)	[aɟént zbulími]
sniper	snajper (m)	[snajpér]

patrol (group)	patrullë (f)	[patrúɫə]
to patrol (vt)	patrulloj	[patruɫój]
sentry, guard	rojë (f)	[rójə]
warrior	luftëtar (m)	[luftətár]
patriot	patriot (m)	[patriót]
hero	hero (m)	[hɛró]
heroine	heroinë (f)	[hɛroínə]

| traitor | tradhtar (m) | [traðtár] |
| to betray (vt) | tradhtoj | [traðtój] |

| deserter | dezertues (m) | [dɛzɛrtúɛs] |
| to desert (vi) | dezertoj | [dɛzɛrtój] |

mercenary	mercenar (m)	[mɛrtsɛnár]
recruit	rekrut (m)	[rɛkrút]
volunteer	vullnetar (m)	[vuɫnɛtár]

dead (n)	vdekur (m)	[vdékur]
wounded (n)	i plagosur (m)	[i plagósur]
prisoner of war	rob lufte (m)	[rob lúftɛ]

112. War. Military actions. Part 1

| war | luftë (f) | [lúftə] |
| to be at war | në luftë | [nə lúftə] |

civil war	luftë civile (f)	[lúftə tsivílɛ]
treacherously (adv)	pabesisht	[pabɛsíʃt]
declaration of war	shpallje lufte (f)	[ʃpáɬjɛ lúftɛ]
to declare (~ war)	shpall	[ʃpaɬ]
aggression	agresion (m)	[agrɛsión]
to attack (invade)	sulmoj	[sulmój]

to invade (vt)	pushtoj	[puʃtój]
invader	pushtues (m)	[puʃtúɛs]
conqueror	pushtues (m)	[puʃtúɛs]

defence	mbrojtje (f)	[mbrójtjɛ]
to defend (a country, etc.)	mbroj	[mbrój]
to defend (against ...)	mbrohem	[mbróhɛm]

enemy	armik (m)	[armík]
foe, adversary	kundërshtar (m)	[kundərʃtár]
enemy (as adj)	armike	[armíkɛ]

| strategy | strategji (f) | [stratɛɟí] |
| tactics | taktikë (f) | [taktíkə] |

order	urdhër (m)	[úrðər]
command (order)	komandë (f)	[komándə]
to order (vt)	urdhëroj	[urðərój]
mission	mision (m)	[misión]
secret (adj)	sekret	[sɛkrét]

| battle, combat | betejë (f) | [bɛtéjə] |
| combat | luftim (m) | [luftím] |

attack	sulm (m)	[sulm]
charge (assault)	sulm (m)	[sulm]
to storm (vt)	sulmoj	[sulmój]
siege (to be under ~)	nën rrethim (m)	[nən rɛθím]

| offensive (n) | sulm (m) | [sulm] |
| to go on the offensive | kaloj në sulm | [kalój nə súlm] |

| retreat | tërheqje (f) | [tərhécjɛ] |
| to retreat (vi) | tërhiqem | [tərhícɛm] |

| encirclement | rrethim (m) | [rɛθím] |
| to encircle (vt) | rrethoj | [rɛθój] |

bombing (by aircraft)	bombardim (m)	[bombardím]
to drop a bomb	hedh bombë	[hɛð bómbə]
to bomb (vt)	bombardoj	[bombardój]
explosion	shpërthim (m)	[ʃpərθím]

shot	e shtënë (f)	[ɛ ʃtə́nə]
to fire (~ a shot)	qëlloj	[cəɬój]
firing (burst of ~)	të shtëna (pl)	[tə ʃtə́na]

| to aim (to point a weapon) | vë në shënjestër | [və nə ʃəɲéstər] |
| to point (a gun) | drejtoj armën | [drɛjtój ármən] |

to hit (the target)	qëlloj	[cəłój]
to sink (~ a ship)	fundos	[fundós]
hole (in a ship)	vrimë (f)	[vrímə]
to founder, to sink (vi)	fundoset	[fundósɛt]

front (war ~)	front (m)	[front]
evacuation	evakuim (m)	[ɛvakuím]
to evacuate (vt)	evakuoj	[ɛvakuój]

trench	llogore (f)	[łogórɛ]
barbed wire	tel me gjemba (m)	[tɛl mɛ ɟémba]
barrier (anti tank ~)	pengesë (f)	[pɛɲésə]
watchtower	kullë vrojtuese (f)	[kúłə vrojtúɛsɛ]

military hospital	spital ushtarak (m)	[spitál uʃtarák]
to wound (vt)	plagos	[plagós]
wound	plagë (f)	[plágə]
wounded (n)	i plagosur (m)	[i plagósur]
to be wounded	jam i plagosur	[jam i plagósur]
serious (wound)	rëndë	[réndə]

113. War. Military actions. Part 2

captivity	burgosje (f)	[burgósjɛ]
to take captive	zë rob	[zə rob]
to be held captive	mbahem rob	[mbáhɛm rób]
to be taken captive	zihem rob	[zíhɛm rob]

concentration camp	kamp përqendrimi (m)	[kamp pərcɛndrími]
prisoner of war	rob lufte (m)	[rob lúftɛ]
to escape (vi)	arratisem	[aratísɛm]

to betray (vt)	tradhtoj	[traðtój]
betrayer	tradhtar (m)	[traðtár]
betrayal	tradhti (f)	[traðtí]

| to execute (by firing squad) | ekzekutoj | [ɛkzɛkutój] |
| execution (by firing squad) | ekzekutim (m) | [ɛkzɛkutím] |

equipment (military gear)	armatim (m)	[armatím]
shoulder board	spaletë (f)	[spalétə]
gas mask	maskë antigaz (f)	[máskə antigáz]

field radio	radiomarrëse (f)	[radiomárəsɛ]
cipher, code	kod sekret (m)	[kód sɛkrét]
secrecy	komplot (m)	[komplót]
password	fjalëkalim (m)	[fjaləkalím]

land mine	minë tokësore (f)	[mínə tokəsórɛ]
to mine (road, etc.)	minoj	[minój]
minefield	fushë e minuar (f)	[fúʃə ɛ minúar]

| air-raid warning | alarm sulmi ajror (m) | [alárm súlmi ajrór] |
| alarm (alert signal) | alarm (m) | [alárm] |

| signal | sinjal (m) | [siɲál] |
| signal flare | sinjalizues (m) | [siɲalizúɛs] |

headquarters	selia qendrore (f)	[sɛlía cɛndrórɛ]
reconnaissance	zbulim (m)	[zbulím]
situation	gjendje (f)	[ɟéndjɛ]
report	raport (m)	[rapórt]
ambush	pritë (f)	[prítə]
reinforcement (army)	përforcim (m)	[pərfortsím]

target	shënjestër (f)	[ʃəɲéstər]
training area	poligon (m)	[poligón]
military exercise	manovra ushtarake (f)	[manóvra uʃtarákɛ]

panic	panik (m)	[paník]
devastation	shkatërrim (m)	[ʃkatərím]
destruction, ruins	gërmadha (pl)	[gərmáða]
to destroy (vt)	shkatërroj	[ʃkatərój]

to survive (vi, vt)	mbijetoj	[mbijɛtój]
to disarm (vt)	çarmatos	[tʃarmatós]
to handle (~ a gun)	manovroj	[manovrój]

| Attention! | Gatitu! | [gatitú!] |
| At ease! | Qetësohu! | [cɛtəsóhu!] |

feat, act of courage	akt heroik (m)	[ákt hɛroík]
oath (vow)	betim (m)	[bɛtím]
to swear (an oath)	betohem	[bɛtóhɛm]

decoration (medal, etc.)	dekoratë (f)	[dɛkorátə]
to award (give a medal to)	dekoroj	[dɛkorój]
medal	medalje (f)	[mɛdáljɛ]
order (e.g. ~ of Merit)	urdhër medalje (m)	[úrðər mɛdáljɛ]

victory	fitore (f)	[fitórɛ]
defeat	humbje (f)	[húmbjɛ]
armistice	armëpushim (m)	[arməpuʃím]

standard (battle flag)	flamur beteje (m)	[flamúr bɛtéjɛ]
glory (honour, fame)	famë (f)	[fámə]
parade	paradë (f)	[parádə]
to march (on parade)	marshoj	[marʃój]

114. Weapons

weapons	armë (f)	[ármə]
firearms	armë zjarri (f)	[ármə zjári]
cold weapons (knives, etc.)	armë të ftohta (pl)	[ármə tə ftóhta]

chemical weapons	armë kimike (f)	[ármə kimíkɛ]
nuclear (adj)	nukleare	[nuklɛárɛ]
nuclear weapons	armë nukleare (f)	[ármə nuklɛárɛ]
bomb	bombë (f)	[bómbə]

atomic bomb	bombë atomike (f)	[bómbə atomíkɛ]
pistol (gun)	pistoletë (f)	[pistolétə]
rifle	pushkë (f)	[púʃkə]
submachine gun	mitraloz (m)	[mitralóz]
machine gun	mitraloz (m)	[mitralóz]
muzzle	grykë (f)	[grýkə]
barrel	tytë pushke (f)	[týtə púʃkɛ]
calibre	kalibër (m)	[kalíbər]
trigger	këmbëz (f)	[kémbəz]
sight (aiming device)	shënjestër (f)	[ʃənéstər]
magazine	karikator (m)	[karikatór]
butt (shoulder stock)	qytë (f)	[cýtə]
hand grenade	bombë dore (f)	[bómbə dórɛ]
explosive	eksploziv (m)	[ɛksplozív]
bullet	plumb (m)	[plúmb]
cartridge	fishek (m)	[fiʃék]
charge	karikim (m)	[karikím]
ammunition	municion (m)	[munitsión]
bomber (aircraft)	avion bombardues (m)	[avión bombardúɛs]
fighter	avion luftarak (m)	[avión luftarák]
helicopter	helikopter (m)	[hɛlikoptér]
anti-aircraft gun	armë anti-ajrore (f)	[ármə ánti-ajrórɛ]
tank	tank (m)	[tank]
tank gun	top tanku (m)	[top tánku]
artillery	artileri (f)	[artilɛrí]
gun (cannon, howitzer)	top (m)	[top]
to lay (a gun)	vë në shënjestër	[və nə ʃənéstər]
shell (projectile)	mortajë (f)	[mortájə]
mortar bomb	bombë mortaje (f)	[bómbə mortájɛ]
mortar	mortajë (f)	[mortájə]
splinter (shell fragment)	copëz mortaje (f)	[tsópəz mortájɛ]
submarine	nëndetëse (f)	[nəndétəsɛ]
torpedo	silurë (f)	[silúrə]
missile	raketë (f)	[rakétə]
to load (gun)	mbush	[mbúʃ]
to shoot (vi)	qëlloj	[cəłój]
to point at (the cannon)	drejtoj	[drɛjtój]
bayonet	bajonetë (f)	[bajonétə]
rapier	shpatë (f)	[ʃpátə]
sabre (e.g. cavalry ~)	shpatë (f)	[ʃpátə]
spear (weapon)	shtizë (f)	[ʃtízə]
bow	hark (m)	[hárk]
arrow	shigjetë (f)	[ʃɟétə]
musket	musketë (f)	[muskétə]
crossbow	pushkë-shigjetë (f)	[púʃkə-ʃɟétə]

115. Ancient people

primitive (prehistoric)	prehistorik	[prɛhistorík]
prehistoric (adj)	prehistorike	[prɛhistoríkɛ]
ancient (~ civilization)	i lashtë	[i láʃtə]

Stone Age	Epoka e Gurit (f)	[ɛpóka ɛ gúrit]
Bronze Age	Epoka e Bronzit (f)	[ɛpóka ɛ brónzit]
Ice Age	Epoka e akullit (f)	[ɛpóka ɛ ákutit]

tribe	klan (m)	[klan]
cannibal	kanibal (m)	[kanibál]
hunter	gjahtar (m)	[ɟahtár]
to hunt (vi, vt)	dal për gjah	[dál pər ɟáh]
mammoth	mamut (m)	[mamút]

cave	shpellë (f)	[ʃpétə]
fire	zjarr (m)	[zjar]
campfire	zjarr kampingu (m)	[zjar kampíŋu]
cave painting	vizatim në shpella (m)	[vizatím nə ʃpéta]

tool (e.g. stone axe)	vegël (f)	[végəl]
spear	shtizë (f)	[ʃtízə]
stone axe	sëpatë guri (f)	[səpátə gúri]
to be at war	në luftë	[nə lúftə]
to domesticate (vt)	zbus	[zbus]

idol	idhull (m)	[íðut]
to worship (vt)	adhuroj	[aðurój]
superstition	besëtytni (f)	[bɛsətytní]
rite	rit (m)	[rit]

evolution	evolucion (m)	[ɛvolutsión]
development	zhvillim (m)	[ʒvitím]
disappearance (extinction)	zhdukje (f)	[ʒdúkjɛ]
to adapt oneself	përshtatem	[pərʃtátɛm]

archaeology	arkeologji (f)	[arkɛoloɟí]
archaeologist	arkeolog (m)	[arkɛológ]
archaeological (adj)	arkeologjike	[arkɛoloɟíkɛ]

excavation site	vendi i gërmimeve (m)	[véndi i gərmímɛvɛ]
excavations	gërmime (pl)	[gərmímɛ]
find (object)	zbulim (m)	[zbulím]
fragment	fragment (m)	[fragmént]

116. Middle Ages

people (ethnic group)	popull (f)	[póput]
peoples	popuj (pl)	[pópuj]
tribe	klan (m)	[klan]
tribes	klane (pl)	[klánɛ]
barbarians	barbarë (pl)	[barbárə]

Gauls	Galët (pl)	[gálət]
Goths	Gotët (pl)	[gótət]
Slavs	Sllavët (pl)	[slávət]
Vikings	Vikingët (pl)	[vikíŋət]

| Romans | Romakët (pl) | [romákət] |
| Roman (adj) | romak | [romák] |

Byzantines	Bizantinët (pl)	[bizantínət]
Byzantium	Bizanti (m)	[bizánti]
Byzantine (adj)	bizantine	[bizantínɛ]

emperor	perandor (m)	[pɛrandór]
leader, chief (tribal ~)	prijës (m)	[príjəs]
powerful (~ king)	i fuqishëm	[i fucíʃəm]
king	mbret (m)	[mbrét]
ruler (sovereign)	sundimtar (m)	[sundimtár]

knight	kalorës (m)	[kalórəs]
feudal lord	lord feudal (m)	[lórd fɛudál]
feudal (adj)	feudal	[fɛudál]
vassal	vasal (m)	[vasál]

duke	dukë (f)	[dúkə]
earl	kont (m)	[kont]
baron	baron (m)	[barón]
bishop	peshkop (m)	[pɛʃkóp]

armour	parzmore (f)	[parzmórɛ]
shield	mburojë (f)	[mburójə]
sword	shpatë (f)	[ʃpátə]
visor	ballnik (m)	[baɫník]
chainmail	thurak (m)	[θurák]

| Crusade | Kryqëzata (f) | [krycəzáta] |
| crusader | kryqtar (m) | [kryctár] |

territory	territor (m)	[tɛritór]
to attack (invade)	sulmoj	[sulmój]
to conquer (vt)	mposht	[mpóʃt]
to occupy (invade)	pushtoj	[puʃtój]

siege (to be under ~)	nën rrethim (m)	[nən rɛθím]
besieged (adj)	i rrethuar	[i rɛθúar]
to besiege (vt)	rrethoj	[rɛθój]

inquisition	inkuizicion (m)	[inkuizitsión]
inquisitor	inkuizitor (m)	[inkuizitór]
torture	torturë (f)	[tortúrə]
cruel (adj)	mizor	[mizór]
heretic	heretik (m)	[hɛrɛtík]
heresy	herezi (f)	[hɛrɛzí]

seafaring	lundrim (m)	[lundrím]
pirate	pirat (m)	[pirát]
piracy	pirateri (f)	[piratɛrí]

boarding (attack)	sulm me anije (m)	[sulm mɛ aníjɛ]
loot, booty	plaçkë (f)	[plátʃkə]
treasure	thesare (pl)	[θɛsárɛ]

discovery	zbulim (m)	[zbulím]
to discover (new land, etc.)	zbuloj	[zbulój]
expedition	ekspeditë (f)	[ɛkspɛdítə]

musketeer	musketar (m)	[muskɛtár]
cardinal	kardinal (m)	[kardinál]
heraldry	heraldikë (f)	[hɛraldíkə]
heraldic (adj)	heraldik	[hɛraldík]

117. Leader. Chief. Authorities

king	mbret (m)	[mbrét]
queen	mbretëreshë (f)	[mbrɛtəréʃə]
royal (adj)	mbretërore	[mbrɛtərórɛ]
kingdom	mbretëri (f)	[mbrɛtərí]

prince	princ (m)	[prints]
princess	princeshë (f)	[printséʃə]

president	president (m)	[prɛsidént]
vice-president	zëvendës president (m)	[zəvéndəs prɛsidént]
senator	senator (m)	[sɛnatór]

monarch	monark (m)	[monárk]
ruler (sovereign)	sundimtar (m)	[sundimtár]
dictator	diktator (m)	[diktatór]
tyrant	tiran (m)	[tirán]
magnate	manjat (m)	[maɲát]

director	drejtor (m)	[drɛjtór]
chief	udhëheqës (m)	[uðəhécəs]
manager (director)	drejtor (m)	[drɛjtór]
boss	bos (m)	[bos]
owner	pronar (m)	[pronár]

leader	lider (m)	[lidér]
head (~ of delegation)	kryetar (m)	[kryɛtár]
authorities	autoritetet (pl)	[autoritétɛt]
superiors	eprorët (pl)	[ɛprórət]

governor	guvernator (m)	[guvɛrnatór]
consul	konsull (m)	[kónsuɫ]
diplomat	diplomat (m)	[diplomát]
mayor	kryetar komune (m)	[kryɛtár komúnɛ]
sheriff	sherif (m)	[ʃɛríf]

emperor	perandor (m)	[pɛrandór]
tsar, czar	car (m)	[tsár]
pharaoh	faraon (m)	[faraón]
khan	khan (m)	[khán]

118. Breaking the law. Criminals. Part 1

bandit	**bandit** (m)	[bandít]
crime	**krim** (m)	[krim]
criminal (person)	**kriminel** (m)	[kriminél]
thief	**hajdut** (m)	[hajdút]
to steal (vi, vt)	**vjedh**	[vjɛð]
stealing, theft	**vjedhje** (f)	[vjéðjɛ]
to kidnap (vt)	**rrëmbej**	[rəmbéj]
kidnapping	**rrëmbim** (m)	[rəmbím]
kidnapper	**rrëmbyes** (m)	[rəmbýɛs]
ransom	**shpërblesë** (f)	[ʃpərblésə]
to demand ransom	**kërkoj shpërblesë**	[kərkój ʃpərblésə]
to rob (vt)	**grabis**	[grabís]
robbery	**grabitje** (f)	[grabítjɛ]
robber	**grabitës** (m)	[grabítəs]
to extort (vt)	**zhvat**	[ʒvat]
extortionist	**zhvatës** (m)	[ʒvátəs]
extortion	**zhvatje** (f)	[ʒvátjɛ]
to murder, to kill	**vras**	[vras]
murder	**vrasje** (f)	[vrásjɛ]
murderer	**vrasës** (m)	[vrásəs]
gunshot	**e shtënë** (f)	[ɛ ʃténə]
to fire (~ a shot)	**qëlloj**	[cətój]
to shoot to death	**qëlloj për vdekje**	[cətój pər vdékjɛ]
to shoot (vi)	**qëlloj**	[cətój]
shooting	**të shtëna** (pl)	[tə ʃténa]
incident (fight, etc.)	**incident** (m)	[intsidént]
fight, brawl	**përleshje** (f)	[pərléʃjɛ]
Help!	**Ndihmë!**	[ndíhmə!]
victim	**viktimë** (f)	[viktímə]
to damage (vt)	**dëmtoj**	[dəmtój]
damage	**dëm** (m)	[dəm]
dead body, corpse	**kufomë** (f)	[kufómə]
grave (~ crime)	**i rëndë**	[i réndə]
to attack (vt)	**sulmoj**	[sulmój]
to beat (to hit)	**rrah**	[rah]
to beat up	**sakatoj**	[sakatój]
to take (rob of sth)	**rrëmbej**	[rəmbéj]
to stab to death	**ther për vdekje**	[θɛr pər vdékjɛ]
to maim (vt)	**gjymtoj**	[ɟymtój]
to wound (vt)	**plagos**	[plagós]
blackmail	**shantazh** (m)	[ʃantáʒ]
to blackmail (vt)	**bëj shantazh**	[bəj ʃantáʒ]

blackmailer	shantazhist (m)	[ʃantaʒíst]
protection racket	rrjet mashtrimi (m)	[rjét maʃtrími]
racketeer	mashtrues (m)	[maʃtrúɛs]
gangster	gangster (m)	[gaŋstér]
mafia	mafia (f)	[máfia]

pickpocket	vjedhës xhepash (m)	[vjéðəs dʒépaʃ]
burglar	hajdut (m)	[hajdút]
smuggling	trafikim (m)	[trafikím]
smuggler	trafikues (m)	[trafikúɛs]

forgery	falsifikim (m)	[falsifikím]
to forge (counterfeit)	falsifikoj	[falsifikój]
fake (forged)	fals	[fáls]

119. Breaking the law. Criminals. Part 2

rape	përdhunim (m)	[pərðuním]
to rape (vt)	përdhunoj	[pərðunój]
rapist	përdhunues (m)	[pərðunúɛs]
maniac	maniak (m)	[maniák]

prostitute (fem.)	prostitutë (f)	[prostitútə]
prostitution	prostitucion (m)	[prostitutsión]
pimp	tutor (m)	[tutór]

| drug addict | narkoman (m) | [narkomán] |
| drug dealer | trafikant droge (m) | [trafikánt drógɛ] |

to blow up (bomb)	shpërthej	[ʃpərθéj]
explosion	shpërthim (m)	[ʃpərθím]
to set fire	vë flakën	[və flákən]
arsonist	zjarrvënës (m)	[zjarvénəs]

terrorism	terrorizëm (m)	[tɛrorízəm]
terrorist	terrorist (m)	[tɛroríst]
hostage	peng (m)	[pɛŋ]

to swindle (deceive)	mashtroj	[maʃtrój]
swindle, deception	mashtrim (m)	[maʃtrím]
swindler	mashtrues (m)	[maʃtrúɛs]

to bribe (vt)	jap ryshfet	[jap ryʃfét]
bribery	ryshfet (m)	[ryʃfét]
bribe	ryshfet (m)	[ryʃfét]

poison	helm (m)	[hɛlm]
to poison (vt)	helmoj	[hɛlmój]
to poison oneself	helmohem	[hɛlmóhɛm]

suicide (act)	vetëvrasje (f)	[vɛtəvrásjɛ]
suicide (person)	vetëvrasës (m)	[vɛtəvrásəs]
to threaten (vt)	kërcënoj	[kərtsənój]
threat	kërcënim (m)	[kərtsəním]

| to make an attempt | tentoj | [tɛntój] |
| attempt (attack) | atentat (m) | [atɛntát] |

| to steal (a car) | vjedh | [vjɛð] |
| to hijack (a plane) | rrëmbej | [rəmbéj] |

| revenge | hakmarrje (f) | [hakmárjɛ] |
| to avenge (get revenge) | hakmerrem | [hakmérɛm] |

to torture (vt)	torturoj	[torturój]
torture	torturë (f)	[tortúrə]
to torment (vt)	torturoj	[torturój]

pirate	pirat (m)	[pirát]
hooligan	huligan (m)	[huligán]
armed (adj)	i armatosur	[i armatósur]
violence	dhunë (f)	[ðúnə]
illegal (unlawful)	ilegal	[ilɛgál]

| spying (espionage) | spiunazh (m) | [spiunáʒ] |
| to spy (vi) | spiunoj | [spiunój] |

120. Police. Law. Part 1

| justice | drejtësi (f) | [drɛjtəsí] |
| court (see you in ~) | gjykatë (f) | [ɟykátə] |

judge	gjykatës (m)	[ɟykátəs]
jurors	anëtar jurie (m)	[anətár juríɛ]
jury trial	gjyq me juri (m)	[ɟýc mɛ jurí]
to judge, to try (vt)	gjykoj	[ɟykój]

lawyer, barrister	avokat (m)	[avokát]
defendant	pandehur (m)	[pandéhur]
dock	bankë e të pandehurit (f)	[bánkə ɛ tə pandéhurit]

| charge | akuzë (f) | [akúzə] |
| accused | i akuzuar (m) | [i akuzúar] |

| sentence | vendim (m) | [vɛndím] |
| to sentence (vt) | dënoj | [dənój] |

guilty (culprit)	fajtor (m)	[fajtór]
to punish (vt)	ndëshkoj	[ndəʃkój]
punishment	ndëshkim (m)	[ndəʃkím]

fine (penalty)	gjobë (f)	[ɟóbə]
life imprisonment	burgim i përjetshëm (m)	[burgím i pərjétʃəm]
death penalty	dënim me vdekje (m)	[dəním mɛ vdékjɛ]
electric chair	karrige elektrike (f)	[karígɛ ɛlɛktríkɛ]
gallows	varje (f)	[várjɛ]

| to execute (vt) | ekzekutoj | [ɛkzɛkutój] |
| execution | ekzekutim (m) | [ɛkzɛkutím] |

| prison | burg (m) | [búrg] |
| cell | qeli (f) | [cɛlí] |

escort (convoy)	eskortë (f)	[ɛskórtə]
prison officer	gardian burgu (m)	[gardián búrgu]
prisoner	i burgosur (m)	[i burgósur]

| handcuffs | pranga (f) | [práŋa] |
| to handcuff (vt) | vë prangat | [və práŋat] |

prison break	arratisje nga burgu (f)	[aratísjɛ ŋa búrgu]
to break out (vi)	arratisem	[aratísɛm]
to disappear (vi)	zhduk	[ʒduk]
to release (from prison)	dal nga burgu	[dál ŋa búrgu]
amnesty	amnisti (f)	[amnistí]

police	polici (f)	[politsí]
police officer	polic (m)	[políts]
police station	komisariat (m)	[komisariát]
truncheon	shkop gome (m)	[ʃkop gómɛ]
megaphone (loudhailer)	altoparlant (m)	[altoparlánt]

patrol car	makinë patrullimi (f)	[makínə patruɫími]
siren	alarm (m)	[alárm]
to turn on the siren	ndez sirenën	[ndɛz sirénən]
siren call	zhurmë alarmi (f)	[ʒúrmə alármi]

crime scene	skenë krimi (f)	[skénə krími]
witness	dëshmitar (m)	[dəʃmitár]
freedom	liri (f)	[lirí]
accomplice	bashkëpunëtor (m)	[baʃkəpunətór]
to flee (vi)	zhdukem	[ʒdúkɛm]
trace (to leave a ~)	gjurmë (f)	[ɟúrmə]

121. Police. Law. Part 2

search (investigation)	kërkim (m)	[kərkím]
to look for ...	kërkoj ...	[kərkój ...]
suspicion	dyshim (m)	[dyʃím]
suspicious (e.g., ~ vehicle)	i dyshuar	[i dyʃúar]
to stop (cause to halt)	ndaloj	[ndalój]
to detain (keep in custody)	mbaj të ndaluar	[mbáj tə ndalúar]

case (lawsuit)	padi (f)	[padí]
investigation	hetim (m)	[hɛtím]
detective	detektiv (m)	[dɛtɛktív]
investigator	hetues (m)	[hɛtúɛs]
hypothesis	hipotezë (f)	[hipotézə]

motive	motiv (m)	[motív]
interrogation	marrje në pyetje (f)	[márjɛ nə pýɛtjɛ]
to interrogate (vt)	marr në pyetje	[mar nə pýɛtjɛ]
to question	pyes	[pýɛs]
(~ neighbors, etc.)		

check (identity ~)	**verifikim** (m)	[vɛrifikím]
round-up (raid)	**kontroll në grup** (m)	[kontróɫ nə grúp]
search (~ warrant)	**bastisje** (f)	[bastísjɛ]
chase (pursuit)	**ndjekje** (f)	[ndjékjɛ]
to pursue, to chase	**ndjek**	[ndjék]
to track (a criminal)	**ndjek**	[ndjék]
arrest	**arrestim** (m)	[arɛstím]
to arrest (sb)	**arrestoj**	[arɛstój]
to catch (thief, etc.)	**kap**	[kap]
capture	**kapje** (f)	[kápjɛ]
document	**dokument** (m)	[dokumént]
proof (evidence)	**provë** (f)	[próvə]
to prove (vt)	**dëshmoj**	[dəʃmój]
footprint	**gjurmë** (f)	[ɟúrmə]
fingerprints	**shenja gishtash** (pl)	[ʃéɲa gíʃtaʃ]
piece of evidence	**provë** (f)	[próvə]
alibi	**alibi** (f)	[alibí]
innocent (not guilty)	**i pafajshëm**	[i pafájʃəm]
injustice	**padrejtësi** (f)	[padrɛjtəsí]
unjust, unfair (adj)	**i padrejtë**	[i padréjtə]
criminal (adj)	**kriminale**	[kriminálɛ]
to confiscate (vt)	**konfiskoj**	[konfiskój]
drug (illegal substance)	**drogë** (f)	[drógə]
weapon, gun	**armë** (f)	[ármə]
to disarm (vt)	**çarmatos**	[tʃarmatós]
to order (command)	**urdhëroj**	[urðərój]
to disappear (vi)	**zhduk**	[ʒduk]
law	**ligj** (m)	[liɟ]
legal, lawful (adj)	**ligjor**	[liɟór]
illegal, illicit (adj)	**i paligjshëm**	[i palíʃʃəm]
responsibility (blame)	**përgjegjësi** (f)	[pərɟɛɟəsí]
responsible (adj)	**përgjegjës**	[pərɟéɟəs]

NATURE

The Earth. Part 1

space	hapësirë (f)	[hapəsírə]
space (as adj)	hapësinor	[hapəsinór]
outer space	kozmos (m)	[kozmós]
world	botë (f)	[bótə]
universe	univers	[univérs]
galaxy	galaksi (f)	[galaksí]
star	yll (m)	[yɫ]
constellation	yllësi (f)	[yɫəsí]
planet	planet (m)	[planét]
satellite	satelit (m)	[satɛlít]
meteorite	meteor (m)	[mɛtɛór]
comet	kometë (f)	[kométə]
asteroid	asteroid (m)	[astɛroíd]
orbit	orbitë (f)	[orbítə]
to revolve	rrotullohet	[rotuɫóhɛt]
(~ around the Earth)		
atmosphere	atmosferë (f)	[atmosférə]
the Sun	Dielli (m)	[diéɫi]
solar system	sistemi diellor (m)	[sistémi diɛɫór]
solar eclipse	eklips diellor (m)	[ɛklíps diɛɫór]
the Earth	Toka (f)	[tóka]
the Moon	Hëna (f)	[hə́na]
Mars	Marsi (m)	[mársi]
Venus	Venera (f)	[vɛnéra]
Jupiter	Jupiteri (m)	[jupitéri]
Saturn	Saturni (m)	[satúrni]
Mercury	Merkuri (m)	[mɛrkúri]
Uranus	Urani (m)	[uráni]
Neptune	Neptuni (m)	[nɛptúni]
Pluto	Pluto (f)	[plúto]
Milky Way	Rruga e Qumështit (f)	[rúga ɛ cúməʃtit]
Great Bear (Ursa Major)	Arusha e Madhe (f)	[arúʃa ɛ máðɛ]
North Star	ylli i Veriut (m)	[ýɫi i vériut]
Martian	Marsian (m)	[marsián]

extraterrestrial (n)	jashtëtokësor (m)	[jaʃtətokəsór]
alien	alien (m)	[alién]
flying saucer	disk fluturues (m)	[dísk fluturúɛs]

spaceship	anije kozmike (f)	[aníjɛ kozmíkɛ]
space station	stacion kozmik (m)	[statsión kozmík]
blast-off	ngritje (f)	[ŋrítjɛ]

engine	motor (m)	[motór]
nozzle	dizë (f)	[dízə]
fuel	karburant (m)	[karburánt]

cockpit, flight deck	kabinë pilotimi (f)	[kabínə pilotími]
aerial	antenë (f)	[anténə]
porthole	dritare anësore (f)	[dritárɛ anəsórɛ]
solar panel	panel solar (m)	[panél solár]
spacesuit	veshje astronauti (f)	[véʃjɛ astronáuti]

| weightlessness | mungesë graviteti (f) | [muŋésə gravitéti] |
| oxygen | oksigjen (m) | [oksiɟén] |

| docking (in space) | ndërlidhje në hapësirë (f) | [ndərlíðjɛ nə hapəsírə] |
| to dock (vi, vt) | stacionohem | [statsionóhɛm] |

observatory	observator (m)	[obsɛrvatór]
telescope	teleskop (m)	[tɛlɛskóp]
to observe (vt)	vëzhgoj	[vəʒgój]
to explore (vt)	eksploroj	[ɛksplorój]

123. The Earth

the Earth	Toka (f)	[tóka]
the globe (the Earth)	globi (f)	[glóbi]
planet	planet (m)	[planét]

atmosphere	atmosferë (f)	[atmosférə]
geography	gjeografi (f)	[ɟɛografí]
nature	natyrë (f)	[natýrə]

globe (table ~)	glob (m)	[glob]
map	hartë (f)	[hártə]
atlas	atlas (m)	[atlás]

Europe	Evropa (f)	[ɛvrópa]
Asia	Azia (f)	[azía]
Africa	Afrika (f)	[afríka]
Australia	Australia (f)	[australía]

America	Amerika (f)	[amɛríka]
North America	Amerika Veriore (f)	[amɛríka vɛriórɛ]
South America	Amerika Jugore (f)	[amɛríka jugórɛ]

| Antarctica | Antarktika (f) | [antarktíka] |
| the Arctic | Arktiku (m) | [arktíku] |

124. Cardinal directions

north	veri (m)	[vɛrí]
to the north	drejt veriut	[dréjt vériut]
in the north	në veri	[nə vɛrí]
northern (adj)	verior	[vɛriór]

south	jug (m)	[jug]
to the south	drejt jugut	[dréjt júgut]
in the south	në jug	[nə jug]
southern (adj)	jugor	[jugór]

west	perëndim (m)	[pɛrəndím]
to the west	drejt perëndimit	[dréjt pɛrəndímit]
in the west	në perëndim	[nə pɛrəndím]
western (adj)	perëndimor	[pɛrəndimór]

east	lindje (f)	[líndjɛ]
to the east	drejt lindjes	[dréjt líndjɛs]
in the east	në lindje	[nə líndjɛ]
eastern (adj)	lindor	[lindór]

125. Sea. Ocean

sea	det (m)	[dét]
ocean	oqean (m)	[ocɛán]
gulf (bay)	gji (m)	[ɟi]
straits	ngushticë (f)	[ŋuʃtítsə]

land (solid ground)	tokë (f)	[tókə]
continent (mainland)	kontinent (m)	[kontinént]

island	ishull (m)	[íʃuɫ]
peninsula	gadishull (m)	[gadíʃuɫ]
archipelago	arkipelag (m)	[arkipɛlág]

bay, cove	gji (m)	[ɟi]
harbour	port (m)	[port]
lagoon	lagunë (f)	[lagúnə]
cape	kep (m)	[kɛp]

atoll	atol (m)	[atól]
reef	shkëmb nënujor (m)	[ʃkəmb nənujór]
coral	koral (m)	[korál]
coral reef	korale nënujorë (f)	[korálɛ nənujórə]

deep (adj)	i thellë	[i θéɫə]
depth (deep water)	thellësi (f)	[θɛɫəsí]
abyss	humnerë (f)	[humnérə]
trench (e.g. Mariana ~)	hendek (m)	[hɛndék]

current (Ocean ~)	rrymë (f)	[rýmə]
to surround (bathe)	rrethohet	[rɛθóhɛt]

| shore | breg (m) | [brɛg] |
| coast | bregdet (m) | [brɛgdét] |

flow (flood tide)	batica (f)	[batítsa]
ebb (ebb tide)	zbaticë (f)	[zbatítsə]
shoal	cekëtinë (f)	[tsɛkətínə]
bottom (~ of the sea)	fund i detit (m)	[fúnd i détit]

wave	dallgë (f)	[dáłgə]
crest (~ of a wave)	kreshtë (f)	[kréʃtə]
spume (sea foam)	shkumë (f)	[ʃkúmə]

storm (sea storm)	stuhi (f)	[stuhí]
hurricane	uragan (m)	[uragán]
tsunami	cunam (m)	[tsunám]
calm (dead ~)	qetësi (f)	[cɛtəsí]
quiet, calm (adj)	i qetë	[i cétə]

| pole | pol (m) | [pol] |
| polar (adj) | polar | [polár] |

latitude	gjerësi (f)	[ɟɛrəsí]
longitude	gjatësi (f)	[ɟatəsí]
parallel	paralele (f)	[paralélɛ]
equator	ekuator (m)	[ɛkuatór]

sky	qiell (m)	[cíɛł]
horizon	horizont (m)	[horizónt]
air	ajër (m)	[ájər]

lighthouse	fanar (m)	[fanár]
to dive (vi)	zhytem	[ʒýtɛm]
to sink (ab. boat)	fundosje	[fundósjɛ]
treasure	thesare (pl)	[θɛsárɛ]

126. Seas & Oceans names

Atlantic Ocean	Oqeani Atlantik (m)	[ocɛáni atlantík]
Indian Ocean	Oqeani Indian (m)	[ocɛáni indián]
Pacific Ocean	Oqeani Paqësor (m)	[ocɛáni pacəsór]
Arctic Ocean	Oqeani Arktik (m)	[ocɛáni arktík]

Black Sea	Deti i Zi (m)	[déti i zí]
Red Sea	Deti i Kuq (m)	[déti i kúc]
Yellow Sea	Deti i Verdhë (m)	[déti i vérðə]
White Sea	Deti i Bardhë (m)	[déti i bárðə]

Caspian Sea	Deti Kaspik (m)	[déti kaspík]
Dead Sea	Deti i Vdekur (m)	[déti i vdékur]
Mediterranean Sea	Deti Mesdhe (m)	[déti mɛsðé]

Aegean Sea	Deti Egje (m)	[déti ɛɟé]
Adriatic Sea	Deti Adriatik (m)	[déti adriatík]
Arabian Sea	Deti Arab (m)	[déti aráb]

Sea of Japan	Deti i Japonisë (m)	[déti i japonísə]
Bering Sea	Deti Bering (m)	[déti bériŋ]
South China Sea	Deti i Kinës Jugore (m)	[déti i kínəs jugórɛ]
Coral Sea	Deti Koral (m)	[déti korál]
Tasman Sea	Deti Tasman (m)	[déti tasmán]
Caribbean Sea	Deti i Karaibeve (m)	[déti i karaíbɛvɛ]
Barents Sea	Deti Barents (m)	[déti barénts]
Kara Sea	Deti Kara (m)	[déti kára]
North Sea	Deti i Veriut (m)	[déti i vériut]
Baltic Sea	Deti Baltik (m)	[déti baltík]
Norwegian Sea	Deti Norvegjez (m)	[déti norvɛɟéz]

127. Mountains

mountain	mal (m)	[mal]
mountain range	vargmal (m)	[vargmál]
mountain ridge	kresht malor (m)	[kréʃt malór]
summit, top	majë (f)	[májə]
peak	maja më e lartë (f)	[mája mə ɛ lártə]
foot (~ of the mountain)	rrëza e malit (f)	[rəza ɛ málit]
slope (mountainside)	shpat (m)	[ʃpat]
volcano	vullkan (m)	[vułkán]
active volcano	vullkan aktiv (m)	[vułkán aktív]
dormant volcano	vullkan i fjetur (m)	[vułkán i fjétur]
eruption	shpërthim (m)	[ʃpərθím]
crater	krater (m)	[kratér]
magma	magmë (f)	[mágmə]
lava	llavë (f)	[łávə]
molten (~ lava)	i shkrirë	[i ʃkrírə]
canyon	kanion (m)	[kanión]
gorge	grykë (f)	[grýkə]
crevice	çarje (f)	[tʃárjɛ]
abyss (chasm)	humnerë (f)	[humnérə]
pass, col	kalim (m)	[kalím]
plateau	pllajë (f)	[płájə]
cliff	shkëmb (m)	[ʃkəmb]
hill	kodër (f)	[kódər]
glacier	akullnajë (f)	[akułnájə]
waterfall	ujëvarë (f)	[ujəvárə]
geyser	gejzer (m)	[gɛjzér]
lake	liqen (m)	[licén]
plain	fushë (f)	[fúʃə]
landscape	peizazh (m)	[pɛizáʒ]
echo	jehonë (f)	[jɛhónə]

alpinist	alpinist (m)	[alpiníst]
rock climber	alpinist shkëmbßinjsh (m)	[alpiníst ʃkəmbiɲʃ]
to conquer (in climbing)	pushtoj majën	[puʃtój májən]
climb (an easy ~)	ngjitje (f)	[nɟítjɛ]

128. Mountains names

The Alps	Alpet (pl)	[alpét]
Mont Blanc	Montblanc (m)	[montblánk]
The Pyrenees	Pirenejet (pl)	[pirɛnéjɛt]

The Carpathians	Karpatet (m)	[karpátɛt]
The Ural Mountains	Malet Urale (pl)	[málɛt urálɛ]
The Caucasus Mountains	Malet Kaukaze (pl)	[málɛt kaukázɛ]
Mount Elbrus	Mali Elbrus (m)	[máli ɛlbrús]

The Altai Mountains	Malet Altai (pl)	[málɛt altái]
The Tian Shan	Tian Shani (m)	[tían ʃáni]
The Pamirs	Malet e Pamirit (m)	[málɛt ɛ pamírit]
The Himalayas	Himalajet (pl)	[himalájɛt]
Mount Everest	Mali Everest (m)	[máli ɛvɛrést]

| The Andes | andet (pl) | [ándɛt] |
| Mount Kilimanjaro | Mali Kilimanxharo (m) | [máli kilimandʒáro] |

129. Rivers

river	lum (m)	[lum]
spring (natural source)	burim (m)	[burím]
riverbed (river channel)	shtrat lumi (m)	[ʃtrat lúmi]
basin (river valley)	basen (m)	[basén]
to flow into ...	rrjedh ...	[rjéð ...]

| tributary | derdhje (f) | [dérðjɛ] |
| bank (river ~) | breg (m) | [brɛg] |

current (stream)	rrymë (f)	[rýmə]
downstream (adv)	rrjedhje e poshtme	[rjéðjɛ ɛ póʃtmɛ]
upstream (adv)	rrjedhje e sipërme	[rjéðjɛ ɛ sípərmɛ]

inundation	vërshim (m)	[vərʃím]
flooding	përmbytje (f)	[pərmbýtjɛ]
to overflow (vi)	vërshon	[vərʃón]
to flood (vt)	përmbytet	[pərmbýtɛt]

| shallow (shoal) | cekëtinë (f) | [tsɛkətínə] |
| rapids | rrjedhë (f) | [rjéðə] |

dam	digë (f)	[dígə]
canal	kanal (m)	[kanál]
reservoir (artificial lake)	rezervuar (m)	[rɛzɛrvuár]
sluice, lock	pendë ujore (f)	[péndə ujórɛ]

water body (pond, etc.)	plan hidrik (m)	[plan hidrík]
swamp (marshland)	kënetë (f)	[kənétə]
bog, marsh	moçal (m)	[motʃál]
whirlpool	vorbull (f)	[vórbuɫ]

stream (brook)	përrua (f)	[pərúa]
drinking (ab. water)	i pijshëm	[i píjʃəm]
fresh (~ water)	i freskët	[i fréskət]

| ice | akull (m) | [ákuɫ] |
| to freeze over (ab. river, etc.) | ngrihet | [ŋríhɛt] |

130. Rivers names

| Seine | Sena (f) | [séna] |
| Loire | Loire (f) | [luaɾ] |

Thames	Temza (f)	[témza]
Rhine	Rajnë (m)	[rájnə]
Danube	Danubi (m)	[danúbi]

Volga	Volga (f)	[vólga]
Don	Doni (m)	[dóni]
Lena	Lena (f)	[léna]

Yellow River	Lumi i Verdhë (m)	[lúmi i vérðə]
Yangtze	Jangce (f)	[jaɲtsé]
Mekong	Mekong (m)	[mɛkóŋ]
Ganges	Gang (m)	[gaŋ]

Nile River	Lumi Nil (m)	[lúmi nil]
Congo River	Lumi Kongo (m)	[lúmi kóŋo]
Okavango River	Lumi Okavango (m)	[lúmi okaváŋo]
Zambezi River	Lumi Zambezi (m)	[lúmi zambézi]
Limpopo River	Lumi Limpopo (m)	[lúmi limpópo]
Mississippi River	Lumi Misisipi (m)	[lúmi misisípi]

131. Forest

| forest, wood | pyll (m) | [pyɫ] |
| forest (as adj) | pyjor | [pyjóɾ] |

thick forest	pyll i ngjeshur (m)	[pyɫ i ɲɟéʃuɾ]
grove	zabel (m)	[zabél]
forest clearing	lëndinë (f)	[ləndínə]

| thicket | pyllëz (m) | [pýɫəz] |
| scrubland | shkurre (f) | [ʃkúrɛ] |

footpath (troddenpath)	shteg (m)	[ʃtɛg]
gully	hon (m)	[hon]
tree	pemë (f)	[pémə]

| leaf | gjeth (m) | [ɟɛθ] |
| leaves (foliage) | gjethe (pl) | [ɟéθɛ] |

fall of leaves	rënie e gjetheve (f)	[rəníɛ ɛ ɟéθɛvɛ]
to fall (ab. leaves)	bien	[bíɛn]
top (of the tree)	maje (f)	[májɛ]

branch	degë (f)	[dégə]
bough	degë (f)	[dégə]
bud (on shrub, tree)	syth (m)	[syθ]
needle (of the pine tree)	shtiza pishe (f)	[ʃtíza píʃɛ]
fir cone	lule pishe (f)	[lúlɛ píʃɛ]

tree hollow	zgavër (f)	[zgávər]
nest	fole (f)	[folé]
burrow (animal hole)	strofull (f)	[strófuɬ]

trunk	trung (m)	[truŋ]
root	rrënjë (f)	[réɲə]
bark	lëvore (f)	[ləvórɛ]
moss	myshk (m)	[myʃk]

to uproot (remove trees or tree stumps)	shkul	[ʃkul]
to chop down	pres	[prɛs]
to deforest (vt)	shpyllëzoj	[ʃpyɬəzój]
tree stump	cung (m)	[tsúŋ]

campfire	zjarr kampingu (m)	[zjar kampíŋu]
forest fire	zjarr në pyll (m)	[zjar nə pyɬ]
to extinguish (vt)	shuaj	[ʃúaj]

forest ranger	roje pyjore (f)	[rójɛ pyjórɛ]
protection	mbrojtje (f)	[mbrójtjɛ]
to protect (~ nature)	mbroj	[mbrój]
poacher	gjahtar i jashtëligjshëm (m)	[ɟahtár i jaʃtəlíɟʃəm]
steel trap	grackë (f)	[grátskə]

| to gather, to pick (vt) | mbledh | [mbléð] |
| to lose one's way | humb rrugën | [húmb rúgən] |

132. Natural resources

natural resources	burime natyrore (pl)	[burímɛ natyrórɛ]
minerals	minerale (pl)	[minɛrálɛ]
deposits	depozita (pl)	[dɛpozíta]
field (e.g. oilfield)	fushë (f)	[fúʃə]

to mine (extract)	nxjerr	[ndzjér]
mining (extraction)	nxjerrje mineralesh (f)	[ndzjérjɛ minɛrálɛʃ]
ore	xehe (f)	[dzéhɛ]
mine (e.g. for coal)	minierë (f)	[miniérə]
shaft (mine ~)	nivel (m)	[nivél]
miner	minator (m)	[minatór]

| gas (natural ~) | gaz (m) | [gaz] |
| gas pipeline | gazsjellës (m) | [gazsjéɫəs] |

oil (petroleum)	naftë (f)	[náftə]
oil pipeline	naftësjellës (f)	[naftəsjéɫəs]
oil well	pus nafte (m)	[pus náftɛ]
derrick (tower)	burim nafte (m)	[burím náftɛ]
tanker	anije-cisternë (f)	[aníjɛ-tsistérnə]

sand	rërë (f)	[rə́rə]
limestone	gur gëlqeror (m)	[gur gəlcɛrór]
gravel	zhavorr (m)	[ʒavór]
peat	torfë (f)	[tórfə]
clay	argjilë (f)	[arɟílə]
coal	qymyr (m)	[cymýr]

iron (ore)	hekur (m)	[hékur]
gold	ar (m)	[ár]
silver	argjend (m)	[arɟénd]
nickel	nikel (m)	[nikél]
copper	bakër (m)	[bákər]

zinc	zink (m)	[zink]
manganese	mangan (m)	[maŋán]
mercury	merkur (m)	[mɛrkúr]
lead	plumb (m)	[plúmb]

mineral	mineral (m)	[minɛrál]
crystal	kristal (m)	[kristál]
marble	mermer (m)	[mɛrmér]
uranium	uranium (m)	[uraniúm]

The Earth. Part 2

weather	moti (m)	[móti]
weather forecast	parashikimi i motit (m)	[paraʃikími i mótit]
temperature	temperaturë (f)	[tɛmpɛratúrə]
thermometer	termometër (m)	[tɛrmométər]
barometer	barometër (m)	[barométər]
humid (adj)	i lagësht	[i lágəʃt]
humidity	lagështi (f)	[lagəʃtí]
heat (extreme ~)	vapë (f)	[vápə]
hot (torrid)	shumë nxehtë	[ʃúmə ndzéhtə]
it's hot	është nxehtë	[əʃtə ndzéhtə]
it's warm	është ngrohtë	[əʃtə ŋróhtə]
warm (moderately hot)	ngrohtë	[ŋróhtə]
it's cold	bën ftohtë	[bən ftóhtə]
cold (adj)	i ftohtë	[i ftóhtə]
sun	diell (m)	[díɛɫ]
to shine (vi)	ndriçon	[ndritʃón]
sunny (day)	me diell	[mɛ díɛɫ]
to come up (vi)	agon	[agón]
to set (vi)	perëndon	[pɛrəndón]
cloud	re (f)	[rɛ]
cloudy (adj)	vranët	[vránət]
rain cloud	re shiu (f)	[rɛ ʃíu]
somber (gloomy)	vranët	[vránət]
rain	shi (m)	[ʃi]
it's raining	bie shi	[bíɛ ʃi]
rainy (~ day, weather)	me shi	[mɛ ʃi]
to drizzle (vi)	shi i imët	[ʃi i ímət]
pouring rain	shi litar (m)	[ʃi litár]
downpour	stuhi shiu (f)	[stuhí ʃíu]
heavy (e.g. ~ rain)	i fortë	[i fórtə]
puddle	brakë (f)	[brákə]
to get wet (in rain)	lagem	[lágɛm]
fog (mist)	mjegull (f)	[mjéguɫ]
foggy	e mjegullt	[ɛ mjéguɫt]
snow	borë (f)	[bórə]
it's snowing	bie borë	[bíɛ bórə]

134. Severe weather. Natural disasters

thunderstorm	stuhi (f)	[stuhí]
lightning (~ strike)	vetëtimë (f)	[vɛtətímə]
to flash (vi)	vetëton	[vɛtətón]
thunder	bubullimë (f)	[bubułímə]
to thunder (vi)	bubullon	[bubułón]
it's thundering	bubullon	[bubułón]
hail	breshër (m)	[bréʃər]
it's hailing	po bie breshër	[po biɛ bréʃər]
to flood (vt)	përmbytet	[pərmbýtɛt]
flood, inundation	përmbytje (f)	[pərmbýtjɛ]
earthquake	tërmet (m)	[tərmét]
tremor, shoke	lëkundje (f)	[ləkúndjɛ]
epicentre	epiqendër (f)	[ɛpicéndər]
eruption	shpërthim (m)	[ʃpərθím]
lava	llavë (f)	[łávə]
twister	vorbull (f)	[vórbuł]
tornado	tornado (f)	[tornádo]
typhoon	tajfun (m)	[tajfún]
hurricane	uragan (m)	[uragán]
storm	stuhi (f)	[stuhí]
tsunami	cunam (m)	[tsunám]
cyclone	ciklon (m)	[tsiklón]
bad weather	mot i keq (m)	[mot i kɛc]
fire (accident)	zjarr (m)	[zjar]
disaster	fatkeqësi (f)	[fatkɛcəsí]
meteorite	meteor (m)	[mɛtɛór]
avalanche	ortek (m)	[orték]
snowslide	rrëshqitje bore (f)	[rəʃcítjɛ bórɛ]
blizzard	stuhi bore (f)	[stuhí bórɛ]
snowstorm	stuhi bore (f)	[stuhí bórɛ]

Fauna

predator	grabitqar (m)	[grabitcár]
tiger	tigër (m)	[tígər]
lion	luan (m)	[luán]
wolf	ujk (m)	[ujk]
fox	dhelpër (f)	[ðélpər]

jaguar	jaguar (m)	[jaguár]
leopard	leopard (m)	[lɛopárd]
cheetah	gepard (m)	[gɛpárd]

black panther	panterë e zezë (f)	[pantérə ɛ zézə]
puma	puma (f)	[púma]
snow leopard	leopard i borës (m)	[lɛopárd i bórəs]
lynx	rrëqebull (m)	[rəcébuɫ]

coyote	kojotë (f)	[kojótə]
jackal	çakall (m)	[tʃakáɫ]
hyena	hienë (f)	[hiénə]

| animal | kafshë (f) | [káfʃə] |
| beast (animal) | bishë (f) | [bíʃə] |

squirrel	ketër (m)	[kétər]
hedgehog	iriq (m)	[iríc]
hare	lepur i egër (m)	[lépur i égər]
rabbit	lepur (m)	[lépur]

badger	vjedull (f)	[vjéduɫ]
raccoon	rakun (m)	[rakún]
hamster	hamster (m)	[hamstér]
marmot	marmot (m)	[marmót]

mole	urith (m)	[uríθ]
mouse	mi (m)	[mi]
rat	mi (m)	[mi]
bat	lakuriq (m)	[lakuríc]

ermine	herminë (f)	[hɛrmínə]
sable	kunadhe (f)	[kunáðɛ]
marten	shqarth (m)	[ʃcarθ]
weasel	nuselalë (f)	[nusɛlálə]
mink	vizon (m)	[vizón]

| beaver | kastor (m) | [kastór] |
| otter | vidër (f) | [vídər] |

horse	kali (m)	[káli]
moose	dre brilopatë (m)	[drɛ brilopátə]
deer	dre (f)	[drɛ]
camel	deve (f)	[dévɛ]

bison	bizon (m)	[bizón]
wisent	bizon evropian (m)	[bizón ɛvropián]
buffalo	buall (m)	[búaɫ]

zebra	zebër (f)	[zébər]
antelope	antilopë (f)	[antilópə]
roe deer	dre (f)	[drɛ]
fallow deer	dre ugar (m)	[drɛ ugár]
chamois	kamosh (m)	[kamóʃ]
wild boar	derr i egër (m)	[dér i égər]

whale	balenë (f)	[balénə]
seal	fokë (f)	[fókə]
walrus	lopë deti (f)	[lópə déti]
fur seal	fokë (f)	[fókə]
dolphin	delfin (m)	[dɛlfín]

bear	ari (m)	[arí]
polar bear	ari polar (m)	[arí polár]
panda	panda (f)	[pánda]

monkey	majmun (m)	[majmún]
chimpanzee	shimpanze (f)	[ʃimpánzɛ]
orangutan	orangutan (m)	[oraŋután]
gorilla	gorillë (f)	[goríɫə]
macaque	majmun makao (m)	[majmún makáo]
gibbon	gibon (m)	[gibón]

elephant	elefant (m)	[ɛlɛfánt]
rhinoceros	rinoqeront (m)	[rinocɛrónt]
giraffe	gjirafë (f)	[ɟiráfə]
hippopotamus	hipopotam (m)	[hipopotám]

| kangaroo | kangur (m) | [kaŋúr] |
| koala (bear) | koala (f) | [koála] |

mongoose	mangustë (f)	[maŋústə]
chinchilla	çinçila (f)	[tʃintʃíla]
skunk	qelbës (m)	[célbəs]
porcupine	ferrëgjatë (m)	[fɛrəɟátə]

137. Domestic animals

cat	mace (f)	[mátsɛ]
tomcat	maçok (m)	[matʃók]
dog	qen (m)	[cɛn]

horse	kali (m)	[káli]
stallion (male horse)	hamshor (m)	[ħamʃór]
mare	pelë (f)	[pélə]

cow	lopë (f)	[lópə]
bull	dem (m)	[dém]
ox	ka (m)	[ka]

sheep (ewe)	dele (f)	[délɛ]
ram	dash (m)	[daʃ]
goat	dhi (f)	[ði]
billy goat, he-goat	cjap (m)	[tsjáp]

| donkey | gomar (m) | [gomár] |
| mule | mushkë (f) | [múʃkə] |

pig	derr (m)	[dɛr]
piglet	derrkuc (m)	[dɛrkúts]
rabbit	lepur (m)	[lépur]

| hen (chicken) | pulë (f) | [púlə] |
| cock | gjel (m) | [ɟél] |

duck	rosë (f)	[rósə]
drake	rosak (m)	[rosák]
goose	patë (f)	[pátə]

| tom turkey, gobbler | gjel deti i egër (m) | [ɟél déti i égər] |
| turkey (hen) | gjel deti (m) | [ɟél déti] |

domestic animals	kafshë shtëpiake (f)	[káfʃə ʃtəpiákɛ]
tame (e.g. ~ hamster)	i zbutur	[i zbútur]
to tame (vt)	zbus	[zbus]
to breed (vt)	rrit	[rit]

farm	fermë (f)	[férmə]
poultry	pulari (f)	[pularí]
cattle	bagëti (f)	[bagətí]
herd (cattle)	kope (f)	[kopé]

stable	stallë (f)	[stáɫə]
pigsty	stallë e derrave (f)	[stáɫə ɛ déravɛ]
cowshed	stallë e lopëve (f)	[stáɫə ɛ lópəvɛ]
rabbit hutch	kolibe lepujsh (f)	[kolíbɛ lépujʃ]
hen house	kotec (m)	[kotéts]

138. Birds

bird	zog (m)	[zog]
pigeon	pëllumb (m)	[pəɫúmb]
sparrow	harabel (m)	[harabél]
tit (great tit)	xhixhimës (m)	[dʒidʒimés]
magpie	laraskë (f)	[laráskə]
raven	korb (m)	[korb]

crow	sorrë (f)	[sórə]
jackdaw	galë (f)	[gálə]
rook	sorrë (f)	[sórə]

duck	rosë (f)	[rósə]
goose	patë (f)	[pátə]
pheasant	fazan (m)	[fazán]

eagle	shqiponjë (f)	[ʃcipóɲə]
hawk	gjeraqinë (f)	[ɟɛracínə]
falcon	fajkua (f)	[fajkúa]
vulture	hutë (f)	[hútə]
condor (Andean ~)	kondor (m)	[kondór]

swan	mjellmë (f)	[mjéɫmə]
crane	lejlek (m)	[lɛjlék]
stork	lejlek (m)	[lɛjlék]

parrot	papagall (m)	[papagáɫ]
hummingbird	kolibri (m)	[kolíbri]
peacock	pallua (m)	[paɫúa]

ostrich	struc (m)	[struts]
heron	çafkë (f)	[tʃáfkə]
flamingo	flamingo (m)	[flamíŋo]
pelican	pelikan (m)	[pɛlikán]

| nightingale | bilbil (m) | [bilbíl] |
| swallow | dallëndyshe (f) | [daɫəndýʃɛ] |

thrush	mëllenjë (f)	[məɫéɲə]
song thrush	grifsha (f)	[grífʃa]
blackbird	mëllenjë (f)	[məɫéɲə]

swift	dallëndyshe (f)	[daɫəndýʃɛ]
lark	thëllëzë (f)	[θəɫézə]
quail	trumcak (m)	[trumtsák]

woodpecker	qukapik (m)	[cukapík]
cuckoo	kukuvajkë (f)	[kukuvájkə]
owl	buf (m)	[buf]
eagle owl	buf mbretëror (m)	[buf mbrɛtərór]
wood grouse	fazan i pyllit (m)	[fazán i pýɫit]
black grouse	fazan i zi (m)	[fazán i zí]
partridge	thëllëzë (f)	[θəɫézə]

starling	gargull (m)	[gárguɫ]
canary	kanarinë (f)	[kanarínə]
hazel grouse	fazan mali (m)	[fazán máli]

| chaffinch | trishtil (m) | [triʃtíl] |
| bullfinch | trishtil dimri (m) | [triʃtíl dímri] |

seagull	pulëbardhë (f)	[puləbárðə]
albatross	albatros (m)	[albatrós]
penguin	penguin (m)	[pɛŋuín]

139. Fish. Marine animals

bream	krapuliq (m)	[krapulíc]
carp	krap (m)	[krap]
perch	perç (m)	[pɛrtʃ]
catfish	mustak (m)	[musták]
pike	mlysh (m)	[mlýʃ]

salmon	salmon (m)	[salmón]
sturgeon	bli (m)	[blí]

herring	harengë (f)	[haréŋə]
Atlantic salmon	salmon Atlantiku (m)	[salmón atlantíku]
mackerel	skumbri (m)	[skúmbri]
flatfish	shojzë (f)	[ʃójzə]

zander, pike perch	troftë (f)	[tróftə]
cod	merluc (m)	[mɛrlúts]
tuna	tunë (f)	[túnə]
trout	troftë (f)	[tróftə]

eel	ngjalë (f)	[ŋjálə]
electric ray	peshk elektrik (m)	[pɛʃk ɛlɛktrík]
moray eel	ngjalë morel (f)	[ŋjálə morél]
piranha	piranja (f)	[piráɲa]

shark	peshkaqen (m)	[pɛʃkacén]
dolphin	delfin (m)	[dɛlfín]
whale	balenë (f)	[balénə]

crab	gaforre (f)	[gafórɛ]
jellyfish	kandil deti (m)	[kandíl déti]
octopus	oktapod (m)	[oktapód]

starfish	yll deti (m)	[yɬ déti]
sea urchin	iriq deti (m)	[iríc déti]
seahorse	kalë deti (m)	[kálə déti]

oyster	midhje (f)	[mídjɛ]
prawn	karkalec (m)	[karkaléts]
lobster	karavidhe (f)	[karavíðɛ]
spiny lobster	karavidhe (f)	[karavíðɛ]

140. Amphibians. Reptiles

snake	gjarpër (m)	[ɟárpər]
venomous (snake)	helmues	[hɛlmúɛs]

viper	nepërka (f)	[nɛpérka]
cobra	kobra (f)	[kóbra]
python	piton (m)	[pitón]
boa	boa (f)	[bóa]
grass snake	kular (m)	[kulár]

| rattle snake | gjarpër me zile (m) | [ʝárpər mɛ zílɛ] |
| anaconda | anakonda (f) | [anakónda] |

lizard	hardhucë (f)	[harðútsə]
iguana	iguana (f)	[iguána]
monitor lizard	varan (m)	[varán]
salamander	salamandër (f)	[salamándər]
chameleon	kameleon (m)	[kamɛlɛón]
scorpion	akrep (m)	[akrép]

turtle	breshkë (f)	[bréʃkə]
frog	bretkosë (f)	[brɛtkósə]
toad	zhabë (f)	[ʒábə]
crocodile	krokodil (m)	[krokodíl]

141. Insects

insect	insekt (m)	[insékt]
butterfly	flutur (f)	[flútur]
ant	milingonë (f)	[miliŋónə]
fly	mizë (f)	[mízə]
mosquito	mushkonjë (f)	[muʃkójɲə]
beetle	brumbull (m)	[brúmbuɫ]

wasp	grerëz (f)	[grérəz]
bee	bletë (f)	[blétə]
bumblebee	greth (m)	[grɛθ]
gadfly (botfly)	zekth (m)	[zɛkθ]

| spider | merimangë (f) | [mɛrimáɲə] |
| spider's web | rrjetë merimange (f) | [rjétə mɛrimáɲɛ] |

dragonfly	pilivesë (f)	[pilivésə]
grasshopper	karkalec (m)	[karkaléts]
moth (night butterfly)	molë (f)	[mólə]

cockroach	kacabu (f)	[katsabú]
tick	rriqër (m)	[ríçər]
flea	plesht (m)	[plɛʃt]
midge	mushicë (f)	[muʃítsə]

locust	gjinkallë (f)	[ʝinkáɫə]
snail	kërmill (m)	[kərmíɫ]
cricket	bulkth (m)	[búlkθ]
firefly	xixëllonjë (f)	[dzidzəɫóɲə]
ladybird	mollëkuqe (f)	[moɫəkúcɛ]
cockchafer	vizhë (f)	[víʒə]

leech	shushunjë (f)	[ʃuʃúɲə]
caterpillar	vemje (f)	[vémjɛ]
earthworm	krimb toke (m)	[krímb tókɛ]
larva	larvë (f)	[lárvə]

Flora

tree	pemë (f)	[pémə]
deciduous (adj)	gjethor	[ɟɛθór]
coniferous (adj)	halor	[halór]
evergreen (adj)	përherë të gjelbra	[pərhérə tə ɟélbra]
apple tree	pemë molle (f)	[pémə mótɛ]
pear tree	pemë dardhe (f)	[pémə dárðɛ]
sweet cherry tree	pemë qershie (f)	[pémə cɛrʃíɛ]
sour cherry tree	pemë qershi vishnje (f)	[pémə cɛrʃí víʃɲɛ]
plum tree	pemë kumbulle (f)	[pémə kúmbutɛ]
birch	mështekna (f)	[məʃtékna]
oak	lis (m)	[lis]
linden tree	bli (m)	[blí]
aspen	plep i egër (m)	[plɛp i égər]
maple	panjë (f)	[páɲə]
spruce	bredh (m)	[brɛð]
pine	pishë (f)	[píʃə]
larch	larsh (m)	[lárʃ]
fir tree	bredh i bardhë (m)	[brɛð i bárðə]
cedar	kedër (m)	[kédər]
poplar	plep (m)	[plɛp]
rowan	vadhë (f)	[váðə]
willow	shelg (m)	[ʃɛlg]
alder	verr (m)	[vɛr]
beech	ah (m)	[ah]
elm	elm (m)	[élm]
ash (tree)	shelg (m)	[ʃɛlg]
chestnut	gështenjë (f)	[gəʃtéɲə]
magnolia	manjolia (f)	[maɲólia]
palm tree	palma (f)	[pálma]
cypress	qiparis (m)	[ciparís]
mangrove	rizoforë (f)	[rizofórə]
baobab	baobab (m)	[baobáb]
eucalyptus	eukalipt (m)	[ɛukalípt]
sequoia	sekuojë (f)	[sɛkuójə]

bush	shkurre (f)	[ʃkúrɛ]
shrub	kaçube (f)	[katʃúbɛ]

| grapevine | hardhi (f) | [harðí] |
| vineyard | vreshtë (f) | [vréʃtə] |

raspberry bush	mjedër (f)	[mjédər]
blackcurrant bush	kaliboba e zezë (f)	[kalibóba ε zézə]
redcurrant bush	kaliboba e kuqe (f)	[kalibóba ε kúcε]
gooseberry bush	shkurre kulumbrie (f)	[ʃkúrε kulumbríε]

acacia	akacie (f)	[akátsiε]
barberry	krespinë (f)	[krεspínə]
jasmine	jasemin (m)	[jasεmín]

juniper	dëllinjë (f)	[dəłíɲə]
rosebush	trëndafil (m)	[trəndafíl]
dog rose	trëndafil i egër (m)	[trəndafíl i égər]

144. Fruits. Berries

| fruit | frut (m) | [frut] |
| fruits | fruta (pl) | [frúta] |

apple	mollë (f)	[mółə]
pear	dardhë (f)	[dárðə]
plum	kumbull (f)	[kúmbuł]

strawberry (garden ~)	luleshtrydhe (f)	[lulεʃtrýðε]
sour cherry	qershi vishnje (f)	[cεrʃí víʃɲε]
sweet cherry	qershi (f)	[cεrʃí]
grape	rrush (m)	[ruʃ]

raspberry	mjedër (f)	[mjédər]
blackcurrant	kaliboba e zezë (f)	[kalibóba ε zézə]
redcurrant	kaliboba e kuqe (f)	[kalibóba ε kúcε]
gooseberry	kulumbri (f)	[kulumbrí]
cranberry	boronica (f)	[boronítsa]

orange	portokall (m)	[portokáł]
tangerine	mandarinë (f)	[mandarínə]
pineapple	ananas (m)	[ananás]
banana	banane (f)	[banánε]
date	hurmë (f)	[húrmə]

lemon	limon (m)	[limón]
apricot	kajsi (f)	[kajsí]
peach	pjeshkë (f)	[pjéʃkə]

| kiwi | kivi (m) | [kívi] |
| grapefruit | grejpfrut (m) | [grεjpfrút] |

berry	manë (f)	[mánə]
berries	mana (f)	[mána]
cowberry	boronicë mirtile (f)	[boronítsə mirtílε]
wild strawberry	luleshtrydhe e egër (f)	[lulεʃtrýðε ε égər]
bilberry	boronicë (f)	[boronítsə]

145. Flowers. Plants

flower	lule (f)	[lúlɛ]
bouquet (of flowers)	buqetë (f)	[bucétə]

rose (flower)	trëndafil (m)	[trəndafíl]
tulip	tulipan (m)	[tulipán]
carnation	karafil (m)	[karafíl]
gladiolus	gladiolë (f)	[gladiólə]

cornflower	lule misri (f)	[lúlɛ mísri]
harebell	lule këmborë (f)	[lúlɛ kəmbórə]
dandelion	luleradhiqe (f)	[lulɛraðícɛ]
camomile	kamomil (m)	[kamomíl]

aloe	aloe (f)	[alóɛ]
cactus	kaktus (m)	[kaktús]
rubber plant, ficus	fikus (m)	[fíkus]

lily	zambak (m)	[zambák]
geranium	barbarozë (f)	[barbarózə]
hyacinth	zymbyl (m)	[zymbýl]

mimosa	mimoza (f)	[mimóza]
narcissus	narcis (m)	[nartsís]
nasturtium	lule këmbore (f)	[lúlɛ kəmbórɛ]

orchid	orkide (f)	[orkidé]
peony	bozhure (f)	[boʒúrɛ]
violet	vjollcë (f)	[vjóɬtsə]

pansy	lule vjollca (f)	[lúlɛ vjóɬtsa]
forget-me-not	mosmëharro (f)	[mosməharó]
daisy	margaritë (f)	[margarítə]

poppy	lulëkuqe (f)	[luləkúcɛ]
hemp	kërp (m)	[kərp]
mint	mendër (f)	[méndər]

lily of the valley	zambak i fushës (m)	[zambák i fúʃəs]
snowdrop	luleborë (f)	[lulɛbórə]

nettle	hithra (f)	[híθra]
sorrel	lëpjeta (f)	[ləpjéta]
water lily	zambak uji (m)	[zambák új i]
fern	fier (m)	[fíɛr]
lichen	likene (f)	[likénɛ]

conservatory (greenhouse)	serrë (f)	[sérə]
lawn	lëndinë (f)	[ləndínə]
flowerbed	kënd lulishteje (m)	[kənd lulíʃtɛjɛ]

plant	bimë (f)	[bímə]
grass	bar (m)	[bar]
blade of grass	fije bari (f)	[fíjɛ bári]

leaf	gjeth (m)	[ɟɛθ]
petal	petale (f)	[pɛtálɛ]
stem	bisht (m)	[biʃt]
tuber	zhardhok (m)	[ʒarðók]

| young plant (shoot) | filiz (m) | [filíz] |
| thorn | gjemb (m) | [ɟémb] |

to blossom (vi)	lulëzoj	[luləzój]
to fade, to wither	vyshket	[výʃkɛt]
smell (odour)	aromë (f)	[arómə]
to cut (flowers)	pres lulet	[prɛs lúlɛt]
to pick (a flower)	mbledh lule	[mbléð lúlɛ]

146. Cereals, grains

grain	drithë (m)	[dríθə]
cereal crops	drithëra (pl)	[dríθəra]
ear (of barley, etc.)	kaush (m)	[kaúʃ]

wheat	grurë (f)	[grúrə]
rye	thekër (f)	[θékər]
oats	tërshërë (f)	[tərʃérə]
millet	mel (m)	[mɛl]
barley	elb (m)	[ɛlb]

maize	misër (m)	[mísər]
rice	oriz (m)	[oríz]
buckwheat	hikërr (m)	[híkər]

pea plant	bizele (f)	[bizélɛ]
kidney bean	groshë (f)	[grófʃə]
soya	sojë (f)	[sójə]
lentil	thjerrëz (f)	[θjérəz]
beans (pulse crops)	fasule (f)	[fasúlɛ]

COUNTRIES. NATIONALITIES

147. Western Europe

Europe	Evropa (f)	[εvrópa]
European Union	Bashkimi Evropian (m)	[baʃkími εvropián]
Austria	Austri (f)	[austrí]
Great Britain	Britani e Madhe (f)	[brítani ε máðε]
England	Angli (f)	[aŋlí]
Belgium	Belgjikë (f)	[bεlɟíkə]
Germany	Gjermani (f)	[ɟεrmaní]
Netherlands	Holandë (f)	[holándə]
Holland	Holandë (f)	[holándə]
Greece	Greqi (f)	[grεcí]
Denmark	Danimarkë (f)	[danimárkə]
Ireland	Irlandë (f)	[irlándə]
Iceland	Islandë (f)	[islándə]
Spain	Spanjë (f)	[spáɲə]
Italy	Itali (f)	[italí]
Cyprus	Qipro (f)	[cípro]
Malta	Maltë (f)	[máltə]
Norway	Norvegji (f)	[norvεɟí]
Portugal	Portugali (f)	[portugalí]
Finland	Finlandë (f)	[finlándə]
France	Francë (f)	[frántsə]
Sweden	Suedi (f)	[suεdí]
Switzerland	Zvicër (f)	[zvítsər]
Scotland	Skoci (f)	[skotsí]
Vatican City	Vatikan (m)	[vatikán]
Liechtenstein	Lichtenstein (m)	[litshtεnstéin]
Luxembourg	Luksemburg (m)	[luksεmbúrg]
Monaco	Monako (f)	[monáko]

148. Central and Eastern Europe

Albania	Shqipëri (f)	[ʃcipərí]
Bulgaria	Bullgari (f)	[buɫgarí]
Hungary	Hungari (f)	[huŋarí]
Latvia	Letoni (f)	[lεtoní]
Lithuania	Lituani (f)	[lituaní]
Poland	Poloni (f)	[poloní]

Romania	Rumani (f)	[rumaní]
Serbia	Serbi (f)	[sɛrbí]
Slovakia	Sllovaki (f)	[słovakí]

Croatia	Kroaci (f)	[kroatsí]
Czech Republic	Republika Çeke (f)	[rɛpublíka tʃékɛ]
Estonia	Estoni (f)	[ɛstoní]

Bosnia and Herzegovina	Bosnje Herzegovina (f)	[bósɲɛ hɛrzɛgovína]
North Macedonia	Maqedonia (f)	[macɛdonía]
Slovenia	Sllovenia (f)	[słovɛnía]
Montenegro	Mali i Zi (m)	[máli i zí]

149. Former USSR countries

| Azerbaijan | Azerbajxhan (m) | [azɛrbajdʒán] |
| Armenia | Armeni (f) | [armɛní] |

Belarus	Bjellorusi (f)	[bjɛłorusí]
Georgia	Gjeorgji (f)	[ɟɛoɟí]
Kazakhstan	Kazakistan (m)	[kazakistán]
Kirghizia	Kirgistan (m)	[kirgistán]
Moldova, Moldavia	Moldavi (f)	[moldaví]

| Russia | Rusi (f) | [rusí] |
| Ukraine | Ukrainë (f) | [ukraínə] |

Tajikistan	Taxhikistan (m)	[tadʒikistán]
Turkmenistan	Turkmenistan (m)	[turkmɛnistán]
Uzbekistan	Uzbekistan (m)	[uzbɛkistán]

150. Asia

Asia	Azia (f)	[azía]
Vietnam	Vietnam (m)	[viɛtnám]
India	Indi (f)	[indí]
Israel	Izrael (m)	[izraél]

China	Kinë (f)	[kínə]
Lebanon	Liban (m)	[libán]
Mongolia	Mongoli (f)	[moŋolí]

| Malaysia | Malajzi (f) | [malajzí] |
| Pakistan | Pakistan (m) | [pakistán] |

Saudi Arabia	Arabia Saudite (f)	[arabía saudítɛ]
Thailand	Tajlandë (f)	[tajlándə]
Taiwan	Tajvan (m)	[tajván]
Turkey	Turqi (f)	[turcí]
Japan	Japoni (f)	[japoní]
Afghanistan	Afganistan (m)	[afganistán]
Bangladesh	Bangladesh (m)	[baŋladéʃ]

| Indonesia | Indonezi (f) | [indonɛzí] |
| Jordan | Jordani (f) | [jordaní] |

Iraq	Irak (m)	[irak]
Iran	Iran (m)	[irán]
Cambodia	Kamboxhia (f)	[kambódʒia]
Kuwait	Kuvajt (m)	[kuvájt]

Laos	Laos (m)	[láos]
Myanmar	Mianmar (m)	[mianmár]
Nepal	Nepal (m)	[nɛpál]
United Arab Emirates	Emiratet e Bashkuara Arabe (pl)	[ɛmirátɛt ɛ baʃkúara arábɛ]

| Syria | Siri (f) | [sirí] |
| Palestine | Palestinë (f) | [palɛstínə] |

| South Korea | Korea e Jugut (f) | [koréa ɛ júgut] |
| North Korea | Korea e Veriut (f) | [koréa ɛ vériut] |

151. North America

United States of America	Shtetet e Bashkuara të Amerikës	[ʃtétɛt ɛ baʃkúara tə amɛríkəs]
Canada	Kanada (f)	[kanadá]
Mexico	Meksikë (f)	[mɛksíkə]

152. Central and South America

Argentina	Argjentinë (f)	[arɟɛntínə]
Brazil	Brazil (m)	[brazíl]
Colombia	Kolumbi (f)	[kolumbí]

| Cuba | Kuba (f) | [kúba] |
| Chile | Kili (m) | [kíli] |

| Bolivia | Bolivi (f) | [boliví] |
| Venezuela | Venezuelë (f) | [vɛnɛzuélə] |

| Paraguay | Paraguai (m) | [paraguái] |
| Peru | Peru (f) | [pɛrú] |

Suriname	Surinam (m)	[surinám]
Uruguay	Uruguai (m)	[uruguái]
Ecuador	Ekuador (m)	[ɛkuadór]

| The Bahamas | Bahamas (m) | [bahámas] |
| Haiti | Haiti (m) | [haíti] |

Dominican Republic	Republika Dominikane (f)	[rɛpublíka dominikánɛ]
Panama	Panama (f)	[panamá]
Jamaica	Xhamajka (f)	[dʒamájka]

153. Africa

Egypt	Egjipt (m)	[ɛɟípt]
Morocco	Marok (m)	[marók]
Tunisia	Tunizi (f)	[tunizí]

Ghana	Gana (f)	[gána]
Zanzibar	Zanzibar (m)	[zanzibár]
Kenya	Kenia (f)	[kénia]
Libya	Libia (f)	[libía]
Madagascar	Madagaskar (m)	[madagaskár]

Namibia	Namibia (f)	[namíbia]
Senegal	Senegal (m)	[sɛnɛgál]
Tanzania	Tanzani (f)	[tanzaní]
South Africa	Afrika e Jugut (f)	[afríka ɛ júgut]

154. Australia. Oceania

| Australia | Australia (f) | [australía] |
| New Zealand | Zelandë e Re (f) | [zɛlándə ɛ ré] |

| Tasmania | Tasmani (f) | [tasmaní] |
| French Polynesia | Polinezia Franceze (f) | [polinɛzía frantsézɛ] |

155. Cities

Amsterdam	Amsterdam (m)	[amstɛrdám]
Ankara	Ankara (f)	[ankará]
Athens	Athinë (f)	[aθínə]
Baghdad	Bagdad (m)	[bagdád]
Bangkok	Bangkok (m)	[baŋkók]
Barcelona	Barcelonë (f)	[bartsɛlónə]

Beijing	Pekin (m)	[pɛkín]
Beirut	Bejrut (m)	[bɛjrút]
Berlin	Berlin (m)	[bɛrlín]
Mumbai (Bombay)	Mumbai (m)	[mumbái]
Bonn	Bon (m)	[bon]

Bordeaux	Bordo (f)	[bordó]
Bratislava	Bratislavë (f)	[bratislávə]
Brussels	Bruksel (m)	[bruksél]
Bucharest	Bukuresht (m)	[bukuréʃt]
Budapest	Budapest (m)	[budapést]

Cairo	Kajro (f)	[kájro]
Kolkata (Calcutta)	Kalkutë (f)	[kalkútə]
Chicago	Çikago (f)	[tʃikágo]
Copenhagen	Kopenhagen (m)	[kopɛnhágɛn]
Dar-es-Salaam	Dar es Salam (m)	[dar ɛs salám]

Delhi	Delhi (f)	[délhi]
Dubai	Dubai (m)	[dubái]
Dublin	Dublin (m)	[dúblin]
Düsseldorf	Dyseldorf (m)	[dysɛldórf]

Florence	Firence (f)	[firéntsɛ]
Frankfurt	Frankfurt (m)	[frankfúrt]
Geneva	Gjenevë (f)	[ɟɛnévə]

The Hague	Hagë (f)	[hágə]
Hamburg	Hamburg (m)	[hambúrg]
Hanoi	Hanoi (m)	[hanói]
Havana	Havana (f)	[havána]
Helsinki	Helsinki (m)	[hɛlsínki]
Hiroshima	Hiroshimë (f)	[hiroʃímə]
Hong Kong	Hong Kong (m)	[hoŋ kóŋ]

Istanbul	Stamboll (m)	[stambóɫ]
Jerusalem	Jerusalem (m)	[jɛrusalém]
Kyiv	Kiev (m)	[kíɛv]
Kuala Lumpur	Kuala Lumpur (m)	[kuála lumpúr]
Lisbon	Lisbonë (f)	[lisbónə]
London	Londër (f)	[lóndər]
Los Angeles	Los Anxhelos (m)	[lós andʒɛlós]
Lyons	Lion (m)	[lión]

Madrid	Madrid (m)	[madríd]
Marseille	Marsejë (f)	[marséjə]
Mexico City	Meksiko Siti (m)	[méksiko síti]
Miami	Majami (m)	[majámi]
Montreal	Montreal (m)	[montrɛál]
Moscow	Moskë (f)	[móskə]
Munich	Munih (m)	[muníh]

Nairobi	Najrobi (m)	[najróbi]
Naples	Napoli (m)	[nápoli]
New York	Nju Jork (m)	[ɲu jork]
Nice	Nisë (m)	[nísə]
Oslo	oslo (f)	[óslo]
Ottawa	Otava (f)	[otáva]

Paris	Paris (m)	[parís]
Prague	Pragë (f)	[prágə]
Rio de Janeiro	Rio de Zhaneiro (m)	[río dɛ ʒanéiro]
Rome	Romë (f)	[rómə]

Saint Petersburg	Shën Petersburg (m)	[ʃən pɛtɛrsbúrg]
Seoul	Seul (m)	[sɛúl]
Shanghai	Shangai (m)	[ʃaɲái]
Singapore	Singapor (m)	[siŋapór]
Stockholm	Stokholm (m)	[stokhólm]
Sydney	Sidney (m)	[sidnéy]

Taipei	Taipei (m)	[taipéi]
Tokyo	Tokio (f)	[tókio]
Toronto	Toronto (f)	[torónto]

Venice	**Venecia** (f)	[vɛnétsia]
Vienna	**Vjenë** (f)	[vjénə]
Warsaw	**Varshavë** (f)	[varʃávə]
Washington	**Uashington** (m)	[vaʃiŋtón]

Printed in Great Britain
by Amazon

30962945R00082